THE GOLDEN TREASURE OF
THE ENTENTE CORDIALE

THE GOLDEN TREASURE OF
THE ENTENTE CORDIALE

Michel Becker - Stephen Clarke
Vincenzo Bianca - Pauline Deysson

ÉDITIONS DE LA CHOUETTE D'OR ®

TABLE OF

Contents

© 2020 ÉDITIONS DE LA CHOUETTE D'OR ®

Responsible editor : ÉDITIONS DE LA CHOUETTE D'OR ® - SOUMAILLE - 19320 - SAINT-MARTIN-LA-MÉANNE.

All rights reserved. Reproduction, even partial, is forbidden.

Legal deposit : February 2021.

Printed in February 2021.

ISBN number: 978-29568629-2-5

Authors of the texts : *Michel BECKER - Stephen CLARKE - Vincenzo BIANCA - Pauline DEYSSON.*

Printed by GRAPHIC SERVICE.

Country of production: Monaco.

Cover: Les Editions De La Chouette D'Or ®

Registered trademarks : Chouette d'Or® , Trésor de l'Entente Cordiale® and Golden Treasure Of The Entente Cordiale®.

A WORLD OF TREASURES

A WORLD OF

treasures

EVEN AS A YOUNG BOY, I SHOWED
A GREAT GIFT FOR TAKING RISKS.

◆ When I was only six or seven, I was fatally attracted to the wooden staircase in the entrance hall of our family home. The building had very high ceilings, so there were a lot of stairs. And whenever my parents were looking the other way, I would grab my brother, and we would drag our bedside rugs to the top of the stairs, which were waxed, polished and smoothed with age. Sitting at the rear of our rugs, we would pull the front edges up and over our legs to form a sort of bobsleigh, then launch ourselves down the stairs, bouncing from one step to the next, laughing like maniacs, the thrill of our favourite sport only slightly tinged with fear. At the bottom of the descent, we had to steer our improvised bobsleigh round a difficult corner, and there were a few bumps and bruises, but never any permanent injury. Even so, if we were caught in the act, punishment was swift, and ranged from "no dessert for you" to a slap on the backside, to a full-blown whipping. My father's hand was a fast as my skin was thick.

Angry and smarting, I would take refuge on the attic floor of our house. And exploring the storerooms, the old maids' rooms, guest bedrooms and bathrooms up there, I made some fascinating discoveries. Behind curtains and wardrobe doors, I found countless forgotten objects that no one had ever bothered to throw out: shiny metal boxes, leather cigar and spectacle cases, malodorous old perfume bottles, medals, gas masks, military helmets and uniforms. To me, these were all mysterious treasures. Then there were huge books of sepia photos telling the story of the Great War, and an unillustrated Mickey and Minnie mouse novel with gold lettering on a red cover that helped me to forget the troubles of my present life. It was up there in the attic that I found a creative outlet. Imagining that I was a law enforcer or treasure-hunter, I travelled to places that my real life could not reach.

Who has never dreamt of digging up a golden treasure?

Most people stop doing this kind of thing as soon as they become adults. But I was different. Part of me has remained a child, forever seeking the joy and wonder of adventure. This is why today I am still capable of taking on impossible challenges and foolhardy risks. I have pursued pipe dreams, followed insane whims, and once I even spent all my savings creating my own treasure. In the eyes of many people, all this has earned me the reputation of a man who will try anything, risk everything, and occasionally succeed. Some say I am adventurous, others that I am a true adventurer. Travelling through uncharted territories, I have often found myself in outlandish situations, facing dead ends, involved in intrigues, plunged into the kind of world where real treasures are to be found.

There is a reason why treasures exist. They are to the imagination what a tax haven is to money: untouchable reserves. People hunt for them, mingling greed with the joy of the chase, while others bury them. The treasures might be the object of a fierce rivalry, or the result of a catastrophe. But sometimes they are simply the fruit of generations of patient accumulation, created by prudent people who have perpetuated tradition by accruing the treasure that will be passed down the family tree.

The first time I ever came face to face with this sort of treasure was in a basement in Paris's Place Vendôme. I was around thirty when I was appointed artistic director of the Boucheron jewellery company. The acting director was called Jean-Thierry. I won't mention his family name. He was getting on in years and wanted to teach me the business so that I could take over from him. He took me into the company's euphemistically named "store room". There, behind reinforced doors, I saw design books full of intricate gouaches and watercolours. He showed me carats by the hundred, a solid-gold electric train set, and robots painting in Monet's Giverny garden or performing mechanical dances while dressed in precious stones and standing on gem-encrusted pedestals. It was the same Jean-Thierry who took me to the upper floors of anonymous Parisian apartment buildings to find hidden workshops where priceless jewels were traded from one expert hand to the next. You could say that he infected me with a kind of gold fever. But at the very least, he crystallized in me a love of rare and precious things, and the deep emotion that they arouse.

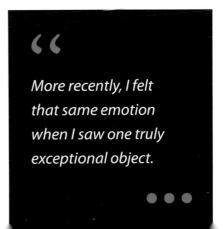

"

More recently, I felt that same emotion when I saw one truly exceptional object.

THE ARENBERG

IT WAS IN A PRIVATE BANK THAT
THIS GRAIL WAS AWAITING ME.

◆ It was in a private bank that this grail was awaiting me. I was not alone. I had come accompanied by specialists to see, or rather to gaze hungrily upon, a forgotten treasure that no one had set eyes on for a century. It was my job to find a buyer for it. All of us present that day felt the same mix of impatience, excitement and awareness of our extreme good fortune.

In the safety deposit box room, my companions helped me pull out a heavy black wooden trunk, in which, swathed in felt coverings, lay a block of white marble. It took two pairs of hands and infinite care to stand it gently on the floor. And there we uncovered the pained, expertly sculpted face of Laocoön, the Trojan priest.

Head of Laocoön.

Before us stood the famous Arenberg Head, a sculpture that had been coveted by some of the great names in history. Ludwig of Bavaria had been willing to give half of his kingdom for it; Napoleon offered a million gold francs. But the Duke of Arenberg refused to let it leave his family, even when he was old, blind and impoverished. In 1909, he invited the archaeologist Ferdinand de Mély to his palace, and on seeing the sculpture, Mély wrote that: "The incisions of the drill and the file to remove chunks of marble were deliberately left rough-cut. Then with confident skill and impeccable judgement, the artist created a startling effect by using crude chisel strokes to hew out splinters of marble. In this way, the most expert hands captured a perfect expression of suffocation that one never feels in other depictions of Laocoön." On first seeing the sculpture, Mély was sure that it was a Michelangelo.

When I first came face to face with this marble jewel, it was a truly intense experience. I travelled back in time to ancient Rome. I felt dizzy in the presence of a treasure that had been uncovered during the excavations at the Vatican. Then I had to leave its present-day Parisian hiding place, the door closed behind me, and I was back in everyday reality.

" On first seeing the sculpture, Mély was sure that it was a Michelangelo.

THE GOLDEN

Owl

SPURRED ON BY MY THIRST FOR
EXTREME SENSATIONS, I CREATED
MY OWN TREASURE.

◆ This was the Golden Owl[1] – in French, la Chouette d'or. It was a nod towards my great-grandfather, Philippe Gustave, known as "le petit Chambord", who was born in 1872, the fruit of one of the Count of Chambord's[2] love affairs. The sculpture also evokes the owl cries of the "Chouans", the loyalists who wanted to restore the monarchy during the French Revolution – "chouan" is an old French word for tawny owl. The Chouette d'or has since achieved a mythical status, embodying the dreams of everyone who has hunted for it, and coming to symbolize the idea of a treasure in the collective imagination.

It took three kilos of gold and 25 of silver to mould the parts that were to be assembled by an expert goldsmith. Since then, time has done its work, and many outrageous stories have been told about the owl. Somewhere out there, a bronze copy of the statue still lies buried, because no one has yet solved the riddles that will eventually guide the treasure hunter to its hiding place.

---

1. Sur la Trace de la Chouette d'Or® (On the Trail of the Golden Owl), published in book form in 1993, was Michel Becker's first treasure hunt. A bronze copy of the owl is buried somewhere in France, and the person who finds it will be able to exchange it for the gold statue.
2. The Count of Chambord was the last legitimate claimant to the French throne. In 1832, his mother, The Duchess of Berry, organized a revolt by anti-revolutionaries in order to establish her son on the throne. The rebels' rallying cry was the hoot of an owl.

The golden owl, made of three kilos of gold, seven kilos of silver and precious stones, will be presented to the winner in exchange for the bronze owl.

In creating the owl, I was typically reckless. I did not have the slightest inkling that it would provoke such strong feelings and extreme behaviour. But fiction gradually became reality. There were plots amongst treasure hunters, secret gatherings, and groups that acted almost like sects. There have been bankrupt publishers and vicious internet rumours, and I have seen people's attitudes harden against me, and become truly insulting. I have seen the game I created turn into serious business that has provoked a media frenzy and genuine fanaticism.

It has been a strange adventure. Max Valentin, who wrote the clues to the treasure hunt, took advantage of my trust in him to try and use the Chouette d'or for his personal self-promotion. However, after setting himself up as a creator of treasure hunts, and going through several bankruptcies, he allowed the owl to be seized by a creditor, and was unable to get it back before he died. It took four years of legal wrangling by my highly talented lawyers before the owl was finally returned to my possession. The affair may have cast doubts on the integrity of the treasure hunt, but I can assure you that the owl is still there. I have seen the gleam in the eye of everyone who has since gazed upon it.

" "

One day I will tell the full story of the Chouette d'or®.

Several kilos of solid gold were used to make the upper layer of the golden owl's wings.

EDWARD VII'S
Golden Casket

IT ALL STARTED ABOUT

TWO YEARS AGO...

◆ **A**fter such a journey, it seemed only natural that this precious casket, commissioned by King Edward VII, should come into my possession. It all started about two years ago, with a simple phone call and an exciting conversation during which I heard about the casket for the very first time.

I knew nothing about Edward VII, an English king famed for his truculence, his sociability and joviality. But I did my research, and learned that he was a lover of fine food and vintage wines, a connoisseur of Paris's ladies of ill repute, as well as being a real friend to France and a generous patron of its arts. If you need convincing, go and look at the Paris theatre that bears his name. Edward is still outside, astride his horse, in a statue sculpted by Paul Landowski.

The golden casket contains a silk-backed parchment inscribed with a long message of friendship from England to France, in the person of Émile Loubet, expressing the importance of the Entente Cordiale between the two countries.

Edward VII's reign was as short as his mother Queen Victoria's was long. When he came to the throne in 1901, he quickly began to work with representatives of the French Republic to further the rapprochement that Victoria had developed with King Louis-Philippe and Emperor Napoléon III of France. The new century had just begun, and the Eiffel Tower was still brand new. However, the French forts defending the Atlantic and Channel coasts against the British fleet had still not been disarmed, except for the redundant Fort Boyard, set between the islands of Aix and Oléron. France was still afraid that it might one day need this intimidating string of defences against English attack. The French defeats against the British fleets, less than a century earlier, were still fresh in the national memory.

At the time, Émile Loubet, the successor to Félix Faure, was President of the Third Republic. It was a period of intense change, packed with historical incident, during which international alliances were considerably reshuffled. One of these changes led to the signing on 8 April 1904 of the bilateral treaty between France and Great Britain that has been immortalized as the Entente Cordiale. With this, hostilities between the two countries were finally at an end, and the first steps towards a united Europe were taken.

I also learned that a year before the treaty, on 7 July 1903, President Loubet had paid a state visit to London as a guest of his friend Edward VII. And that during a great banquet given in his honour at London's Guildhall, Loubet had been presented with a golden casket celebrating the imminent Entente Cordiale. The banquet was a magnificent occasion, coloured by splendid uniforms and official regalia, and organized with the kind of pomp and ceremony

Le Petit Journal

Le Petit Journal
CHAQUE JOUR — SIX PAGES — 5 CENTIMES

Le Supplément illustré
CHAQUE SEMAINE 5 CENTIMES

5 Centimes

SUPPLÉMENT ILLUSTRÉ
Huit pages

L'AGRICULTURE MODERNE, 5 cent. —∗— La Mode du Petit Journal, 10 cent.

5 Centimes

ABONNEMENTS

	SIX MOIS	UN AN
SEINE ET SEINE-ET-OISE	2 fr.	3 fr. 50
DÉPARTEMENTS	2 fr.	4 fr.
ÉTRANGER	2 50	5 fr.

Quatorzième année   DIMANCHE 12 JUILLET 1903   Numéro 660

VOYAGE DU PRÉSIDENT DE LA RÉPUBLIQUE A LONDRES
Le banquet du Guildhall

The Petit Journal - 1903.

LE LORD-MAIRE REMET A M. LOUBET UN COFFRET D'OR

Supplément illustré du Petit Journal

The Petit Journal - 1903.

that only the British know how to deliver.

In illustrations published soon afterwards in the *Petit Journal*, one can see the Lord Mayor of London, Sir Marcus Samuel, handing the golden casket to the French President. It subsequently became a Loubet family treasure, and for over a century it was never seen in public again. Like the Arenberg head, it became a forgotten heirloom.

Then, on 17 January 2017, almost exactly 114 years after it was presented to Loubet, it came to light again, in an auction catalogue. However, as a museum piece, appearing from nowhere, deprived of its historical context, it did not attract a buyer. This was fortunate, though, because in all likelihood it would have disappeared from public view again, this time forever.

I was not present at the sale, and it took me a whole year to track down its owner. Hindered by the discretion and secrecy that are common in such cases, I had to twist, turn, observe and negotiate, before I finally managed to set my eyes on the treasure.

Manufactured by the prestigious Goldsmiths & Silversmiths Company, jewellers by appointment to the Crown, it is part of an age-old London tradition, one of a series of caskets presented to visiting dignitaries. Queen Victoria would present one whenever she visited a newly created borough of London. Sultan Abdulaziz of Turkey received a similar casket in 1867, as did the Canadian Prime Minister Richard Bedford, in 1930. And all of them are now in museums – except the one presented to Émile Loubet.

Inside the casket, cushioned on its satin lining, is a silk-backed roll of parchment, decorated with richly coloured illuminations and inscribed in fine calligraphy with a text celebrating Franco-British friendship. The outer faces of the casket are encrusted with four finely painted porcelain miniatures representing the Palace of Westminster, St Paul's Cathedral, the Royal Opera House and Tower Bridge. The front bears the arms of the City of London, the crossed flags of France and Great Britain, and the enamelled initials of Émile Loubet. On the rear is a plaque engraved with a dedication to Loubet from the City of London. And on the lid, topping the whole thing off, is a golden sculpture, the allegorical figure of Peace crowning France and Britain with laurels.

Now it is time to bring the casket centre-stage, and to evoke its full historic significance. It is time for the casket to emerge from the shadows and deliver its message of peace and hope across political borders and individual memories. It is time for the casket to become immortal.

———— *MICHEL BECKER*

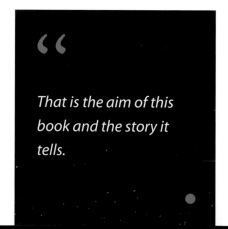

That is the aim of this book and the story it tells.

1218   **King Edward VII. and President Loubet.**
London, July 6, 1903.   *Copyright*

Postcard- Émile Loubet & Edward VII

edward

EDWARD VII, ÉMILE LOUBET AND THE GOLDEN CASKET

EDWARD VII, ÉMILE LOUBET AND

the Golden Casket

THE ENTENTE CORDIALE,
THE TREATY THAT RE-SHAPED EUROPE

In 1902, the world was on the brink of world war. Not the Great War that was to break out in 1914 – this was the danger of an immediate conflict. Amongst all the European heads of state, only the King of England, Edward VII, and the president of France, Émile Loubet, seemed to be genuinely opposed to the idea of war. And even though it sounds absurd, the two leaders were obliged to keep their pacifism secret.

The prime reason for the threat of war was the personality of the German Kaiser, Wilhelm II – who was Edward VII's nephew and the grandson of the former Queen of England, Victoria. Wilhelm had suffered from severe psychological problems ever since childhood and had always shown himself capable of outbursts of impulsive and arrogant behaviour, both in his private and political life.

Unser Kaiserpaar in England.
König Eduard und der Kaiser auf der Jagd in Windsor.

Edward VII and Wilhelm II.

A deeply ambitious man with something of an inferiority complex, the Kaiser was desperate for Germany to become a colonial power, with himself as ruler of a great empire like those of France and Britain. Wilhelm had identified two simple solutions to this German inferiority: first, build up a massive army and naval fleet, and then attack an existing empire – France's for example, which at the time covered large areas of North and West Africa and Asia.

To this end, the Kaiser decided to embroil his uncle Edward VII and his cousin Tsar Nicholas II of Russia – another of Victoria's grandsons – in a family alliance. Wilhelm's plan was to unite Germany, Great Britain and Russia against a single enemy: France. Such a powerful trio would easily overrun not just the French colonies, but also France itself, exactly as an invading Germany army had done in 1870, putting an end to Napoléon III's Second Empire régime.

An Anglo-Russo-German alliance was a real possibility in 1902, because for the previous few years relations between the French and the British had been, as so often throughout their history, awful.

First in 1898, the two nations' rush to colonize Africa had provoked a dangerous confrontation in Sudan. The British were trying to open a north–south corridor of territory between their colonies in Egypt and South Africa, while the French were working at right angles to the Brits, pushing for a chain of colonies from Senegal in the west to Djibouti in the east.

In September 1898, their colonial paths crossed, when two military expeditions met at Fashoda, a small desert fortress nestling on the Nile some 650 kilometres north of Khartoum, the capital of the Sudan. For seven weeks, French troops occupied the fort while a small British army asked them – politely – to vacate the premises.

The leader of each expedition asked their government for advice, and Paris and London were soon exchanging heated messages about the confrontation.

France's Foreign Minister, Théophile Delcassé, asked the British ambassador to Paris, Sir Edmund Monson: "You would not use Fashoda as a cause for the breakdown of relations between us?" (By "breakdown", of course, he meant war.) Monson replied bluntly: "Yes."

At the time, British patriotism was at fever pitch, whipped up even further than usual by the celebration of Queen Victoria's 60th jubilee in 1897. The British public would have supported its government and its army against any opponent in the world – and especially the hereditary enemy, France.

While the diplomats exchanged words about Fashoda, the British fleet was more demonstrative, and held military manœuvres just offshore of the French ports of Brest in Brittany and Bizerte in Tunisia (then a French colony). This was an open threat, and there was clearly a genuine risk of a return to the Anglo-French enmity of the Napoleonic wars.

Looking on gleefully from Germany, Kaiser Wilhelm reportedly commented that: "The situation could become interesting."

In the end, the French thought it wise to make a strategic withdrawal, and the French troops marched out of Fashoda.[1] Colonial conflict had been narrowly avoided, but the French people viewed the whole incident as a humiliation, and a wave of anti-British feeling swept the country. This became a veritable tsunami a year later when Britain started a war against the Boers, the mainly Dutch-speaking immigrants in a part of South Africa that was resisting British attempts to colonize the whole region. Some of the Boers were of French origin (mainly the descendants of Huguenots who had fled religious persecution in the seventeenth century), which gave France an excellent opportunity to wade in on the Boers' side.

An editorialist at French newspaper *Le Figaro* was ecstatic about the war: "The Boers have shown us how decent people fight to defend their independence, and how patriotic unity can inspire them with the fervour necessary for suffering and sacrifice."

But French journalists did more than attack politicians and generals. Some of them

---

1. The Brits subsequently forgot the incident almost entirely and hardly anyone in Britain has heard of Fashoda, but even today, if one mentions the F-word to a French historian, the wound is as raw as the burning of Joan of Arc.

turned on the future King Edward VII himself (who in 1899 was still Prince of Wales, heir to the throne). A satirical magazine, *L'Assiette au Beurre*, published a wickedly mocking caricature of Britannia sporting a tattoo of Edward's face on her buttocks.

Feelings were running so high that in 1900, Edward refused an invitation to the Exposition Universelle de Paris – the first time he had missed one of the city's great trade and science fairs since 1855. In 1899 he had been the guest of honour, so this refusal in 1900 was the symptom of a drastic downturn in Franco-British relations, as well as being a slap in the face for the newly elected President of France, Émile Loubet.

The Boer War continued off and on until 1902, provoking constant opposition from the French, whose attitude quickly turned many British politicians, as well as a large proportion of the British population, into stalwart Francophobes.

It was inevitable that Kaiser Wilhelm would seize upon these increased tensions as an opportunity to pursue his idea of a family alliance against France.

Some powerful Brits were in total agreement with the German leader. The press baron Lord Northcliffe, founder of the *Daily Mirror* and the *Daily Mail*, wrote that: "England hesitated for a long time between France and Germany, but she always respected the German character, whereas she has come to regard France with contempt. An *Entente Cordiale* cannot exist between England and her nearest neighbour. Enough of France, which has neither courage nor political sense."

Lord Lansdowne, the British Secretary of State for Foreign Affairs, was in favour of war against France. He was distrustful of the French and feared that their North African naval bases could be used for an attack on Britain's enclave of Gibraltar. If France captured that strategic outpost, the French navy would dominate the entrance to the Mediterranean. Lansdowne thought that war was practically an obligation.

Fortunately for France and peace, when Edward VII ascended the British throne in 1901, he did not share these anti-French sentiments. And for a very good reason …

Edward was a staunch Francophile, despite being three-quarters German. His father, Prince Albert, was from the German duchy of Saxe-Coburg and Gotha, while his mother Victoria had a British father but a German mother, Victoria of Saxe-Coburg-Saalfeld.

During Edward's whole childhood, Victoria and Albert did their best to turn their son into a miniature German – Teutonically disciplined and morally rigid. But Edward always resisted. Then, in 1855, during a state visit to Paris with his parents, the teenager had a revelation. Young Edward met Emperor Napoléon III and his seductive wife Eugénie, who showed the boy more warmth and affection than Victoria and Albert had ever done, and revealed to him that a royal palace could be a place of entertainment, rather than just being a Teutonic training ground. The adolescent English prince became an instant Francophile.

Later, from the age of 21, Edward, heir to the British throne, made France his second home. His countless escapades in Paris and at Napoléon III's chateaux became infamous. His love of France was first and foremost a fondness for French women – and his many mistresses were not just aristocrats, but also famous actresses like Sarah Bernhardt, cabaret artists like the can-can dancer La Goulue, and high-class prostitutes. Edward did not let class-consciousness get in the way of an erotic encounter.

Several times, his mother, Queen Victoria, tried to forbid him from going to France, but he usually managed to sidestep her attempts to lead him out of temptation. Edward's morals may have been seriously flawed, but in political terms his determination to pursue his taste for all things French had one enormous advantage: when he succeeded to the throne in 1901, Britain had a monarch who could speak fluent French, actually *liked* France, and understood its people's mentality.

This was because, as a young man in France, he had not only frequented actresses' dressing rooms and luxury brothels, he had also rubbed shoulders with the whole spectrum of French politicians – Bonapartists, royalists and republicans. As an honoured guest in France, he had been able to meet politicians without getting bogged down in the politics of the day, so he was liked and respected by such diverse political personalities as the Emperor Napoléon III, Henri d'Orléans (the great-grandson of King Louis-Philippe) and the radical leftist Léon Gambetta, who was a grocer's son.

Edward was therefore not at all prejudiced against a president like Émile Loubet, who was of peasant stock and a devout republican. To Edward, France had always represented *Liberté* and *Egalité*: it was a place where he could be the public lover of a Parisian can-can dancer and the friend of a left-wing president. Back in England, basic snobbery would have made such relations much more difficult, or downright impossible.

So in 1902, the recently crowned King Edward VII did not share the Francophobia expressed by the British people, its "patriotic" newspapers and many of its politicians. He was determined to maintain good relations with France. And despite his own German origins, he felt a deep distrust of his nephew, the bellicose and unstable Kaiser Wilhelm.

Thanks to Edward, then, there was a chance that war between Britain and France could be avoided.

Across the Channel, Edward had a staunch ally in President Émile Loubet, a veteran warhorse of French politics. Loubet had begun his political career in 1870, as mayor of the town of Montélimar in the Drôme, the *département* where he was born. Later, he became the local MP and a senator, and then served as Minister of the Interior and Prime Minister, before coming to office as President in 1899 after the sudden death of Félix Faure, whose heart had failed during an assignation with his mistress.

A political survivor, Loubet was renowned as a man of negotiation and conciliation. The end of the nineteenth century was a highly unstable period in French politics, with divisions between monarchists and republicans, clerical and secular lobbies, and the two sides in the Dreyfus affair. But Loubet had always worked to abate tensions and keep the country on track. He believed that a nation progresses in a climate of social harmony, which was exactly Edward's philosophy.

Also, just like Edward, Loubet wanted to be seen as a leader who was close to his people. The President invited every mayor of a French town or village to the 1900 *Exposition Universelle de Paris* (the one that Edward missed), and organized a huge banquet for them in the Tuileries Gardens, at which 22,965 guests of all political persuasions sat down together for a meal. It was an occasion that the *bon vivant* Edward would have loved.

Émile Loubet

Edward VII

Loubet was already working actively to protect European peace before Edward inherited his throne. In 1900, France signed an alliance with Italy, and then – even more importantly – the following year made a treaty with Tsar Nicholas II of Russia.

Loubet recognized Edward as a long-term ally of France. He and Edward were of the same generation – the former was born in 1838, the latter in 1841 – and the French President knew that Edward had always shown his support for France throughout its political and economic crises following the Franco-Prussian War of 1870-71. As soon as peace returned to France, so did Edward, becoming a frequent visitor to Paris and the French Riviera, both for his own amusement and to help France recover its image as a tourist destination and cultural hub.

Edward was an active participant in France's transformation into the capital of the *Belle Époque*. In 1889, when Edward's mother Queen Victoria forbade him from visiting the *Exposition Universelle* celebrating the centenary of the French Revolution (not exactly a pro-monarchist event, in her opinion), Edward had defied her and attended as a private citizen. It was a gesture of friendship and support that earned the respect and gratitude of French politicians like Loubet.

So when political conflict reared its head again in 1902, the two heads of state were determined to make a similar grand gesture, but a reciprocal one this time. Now, instead of defying Queen Victoria, they would have to stand up against public opinion on both sides of the Channel, where Franco-British hostilities were being whipped up by politicians calling themselves patriots.

Other leaders might have surfed the waves of xenophobia in their respective countries, but King Edward and President Loubet decided to stand together with their sights fixed on a more harmonious horizon. Both of them thought that enmity between Britain and France was an historical throwback. It was time to put Agincourt and the Napoleonic Wars to bed.

Together, therefore, the two men conceived a plan – in almost complete secrecy – to change public opinion on both sides of the Channel and thereby improve the diplomatic situation between Britain and France.

Edward VII already had a date in his 1903 diary to sail the royal yacht *Victoria and Albert* down to Lisbon and visit King Carlos of Portugal. From there, he was due to prolong his cruise with a *buon giorno* to King Victor Emmanuel in Rome (a newfound ally of France). But now Edward also began to plan a "chance" meeting en route with Émile Loubet.

Discretion was vital. If French or British populists got wind of the plan, Edward would be exposed as a sovereign who ignored his ministers and plotted behind their backs. He might find himself excluded from active political life in his country – which was what his mother Victoria had always wanted. She had always thought him too frivolous to be a serious politician. Edward therefore told neither his Foreign Secretary, Lord Lansdowne, nor even his private secretary about the planned meeting with the French president. After some hesitation, he did inform his ambassador in Paris, Sir Edmund Monson, who went to see Loubet, and returned with a reassuring message: the plan could go ahead.

Loubet had apparently told Monson that he "could not over-emphasize the influence that a visit from Edward would have on Franco-British friendship. As Prince of Wales, His Majesty earned exceptional popularity in France, and if he came back, he would see that his reception would be even more affectionate than ever." The memories of Edward's frequent trips to France after 1870 were clearly still fresh in Loubet's mind, and he wanted to renew that atmosphere of open friendship.

So Edward set sail for Portugal and Italy, and when, in April 1903, the royal yacht entered the Mediterranean, the captain received news that President Loubet was in Algiers. What a lucky coincidence…

In fact, Loubet was in North Africa to underline France's presence in the region, and he had arrived there with a battleship called the *Joan of Arc* – which under other circumstances might not have boded too well for Anglo-French relations.

On the evening of 20 April, a grand ball was organized in Algiers in honour of the French navy and its foreign counterparts present there. Several foreign naval vessels were at anchor in the harbour – under Russian, Italian, Spanish and British flags. That evening, the orchestra played all of those national anthems along with the *Marseillaise*. It was an evening of international harmony, both musical and political – but one that notably excluded Germany.

Loubet's mission in Algeria was openly diplomatic: the French press reported that he "conquered all hearts with his cordial personality and his charming naturalness" – which was almost exactly what the same newspapers used to say about Edward during his trips to France. However, no one seemed to have suspected that Loubet's visit had a second, more secret, purpose.

When Edward heard about Loubet's presence in Algiers, as a mark of respect he sent a couple of gunboats to salute the President. In reply, the courteous Frenchman quite naturally invited the King to visit him in Paris on his way home to London. *Excellente idée*, Edward answered, and informed his government that he would be going to France. After all, this invitation was a sign that the French wanted to negotiate about the tensions in the

Mediterranean, so Edward couldn't really refuse, could he? Lansdowne tried to argue, but the King put his foot down and the Foreign Secretary had to give in. The politician didn't yet realize it, but he had been outwitted by the new King of British diplomacy.

The royal visit to Paris was arranged for the beginning of May, just a few days later. The sense of urgency was palpable. There was only one problem: in reality, Loubet had exaggerated when he talked about Edward VII's "exceptional popularity" in France. That same month, an anti-British newspaper called *La Patrie* (*The Homeland*) published two special issues listing every Anglo-French conflict since Joan of Arc, ending with the recent humiliation at Fashoda. A publication called *L'Autorité* (*Authority*) declared that the idea of Edward VII's state visit to France "shocks, offends and revolts us patriots". Meanwhile, postcards went on sale in France showing Napoleon shaking his fist at King Edward and President Loubet, growling, "If only I were still alive."

Even Paris's cabaret artists, who had previously been amongst Edward's biggest fans, joined in the fun. One of them wrote a song with an obscene pun in the title: literally, "*Les Anglais débarquent*" means "the English disembark" but it is also a vulgar euphemism for the start of a woman's period (because of English soldiers' scarlet uniforms).

Another singer had a hit with a number that went "*Edouard sept, gros et gras*": literally

"Edward VII, fat and fat" – *gros* is a word describing the shape of an obese person and *gras* the fattiness of their flesh.

Fortunately, President Loubet was an experienced political strategist, and knew how to deal with this antagonism. He and his Minister of Foreign Affairs, Théophile Delcassé (a former journalist), lobbied the press to try and moderate French public opinion. They even seem to have converted *Le Figaro*'s previously anti-British editorialist: on 1 May 1903, the day Edward arrived in Paris, *Le Figaro* warned that the revolutionary French people "always worry what is hidden in the thoughts of kings". However, clearly following Loubet and Delcassé's official line, the editorialist went on to say that King Edward had "no other idea, no other desire, than to ensure world peace. He is related to all the sovereigns of Europe, most of them younger than he is, and you can be sure that he will use the authority of his age and the familiarity of his family ties to smooth away any obstacles, if there are any, and live in perfect understanding with everyone. It is a great role, a beautiful role."

The problem was that most Parisians either didn't read *Le Figaro* or didn't agree with its editorials. And some British journalists were just as sceptical: *The Times* announced that Edward's visit to Paris was to be a mere formality, of no political importance. It was clear that Loubet and Edward still had a lot of ground to make up.

At 2.55 pm on May Day, King Edward, attired for the occasion in a plumed hat and British general's scarlet jacket, arrived by train at the now-defunct Bois de Boulogne railway station just outside Paris. There he was met by Loubet who, the papers noted, was looking suntanned after his recent trip to North Africa. The two men shook hands, but made no speeches at the station. This was highly unusual: in the past, even when Edward had arrived in Cannes on a simple pleasure trip, the mayor of the city had made a flattering speech on the railway platform.

Now, though, there was no grand welcoming ceremony. This was because there were serious worries about the reception Edward would receive from the Parisian crowd. An assassination attempt was a real possibility. Three years earlier, in 1900, a young Belgian anarchist had shot at Edward and his wife Alexandra at Brussels Station as a protest against the Boer Wars. A bullet had grazed Edward's forehead.

In May 1903, at this vital juncture in Franco-British politics, Émile Loubet did not want to give Parisians any shooting practice. So after swift *bonjours*, the two men climbed into the President's state carriage and drove into central Paris – at least that way they presented a moving target, guarded by a triple rank of Republican Guards on horseback.

Large crowds lined the route. *Le Figaro* reported that these spectators had been waiting for "only" two hours, whereas a decade earlier the Parisians would have been out at dawn to greet Edward, their favourite Englishman.

Driving along the Champs-Élysées, there were shouts of *"Vivent les Boers!"*, *"Vive Fachoda!"* and even *"Vive Jeanne d'Arc!"* When one of Edward's staff moaned that "the French don't like us," the King replied, "Why should they?"

In general, though, the Parisians seemed well disposed towards their royal guest. Plenty of buildings along the route had been decorated with British flags and "Welcome" signs in French and English.

At 5pm, Edward had a brief meeting – just half an hour – with Émile Loubet at the Élysée Palace (the presidential residence), during which they no doubt took the time to congratulate each other on the success of their ruse in organizing Edward's trip, and to run through the timetable of official events, which was going to be intense.

Edward then went to the British Embassy (just along the street) to meet members of the British Chamber of Commerce. Amongst them he had a great ally, a businessman called Thomas Barclay who had long been trying to forge closer commercial links between Britain and France. In 1900, when relations were at a low-point, Barclay had invited five hundred British entrepreneurs to the *Exposition Universelle de Paris*. So Edward was assured of a favourable reception when he gave a speech to the British Chamber of Commerce about Anglo-French friendship, expressing his hope that Britain and France could end their hostilities and work together as "champions and pioneers of civilization and peaceful progress". Naturally, the speech was released to the French press to be published the next day.

After a twelve-course dinner at the British Embassy that featured a diplomatic mixture of dishes – cream of asparagus soup *à la Reine*, followed by fillet of beef *à l'anglaise* with *petits pois à la française* – Edward went out to the Théâtre Français to see a play about a man who falls in love with an ex, only to become infatuated with her daughter. Typically Parisian fodder.

There was drama even before the play began, however. Unlike past outings to the Parisian theatre, when Edward would be cheered merely for his choice of mistress that evening, there was a heavy silence amongst the audience as the King took his seat. Even the pro-British newspaper *Le Figaro* reported nothing more than a "murmur of curiosity".

Edward guffawed through the first act and then, during the interval, he strolled out into the corridors with the rest of the audience, followed closely by his anxious police bodyguards. There, apparently by chance, the King bumped into someone he knew: it was a former star of the Paris stage, and an ex-lover of his, Jeanne Granier, now in her early fifties. But was it really a chance meeting? Almost certainly not.

7 Juillet 1903

Consommé Renaissance

Crème Alexandra

Cantaloups frappés au Porto

Truite Saumonée Vénitienne

Selle d'Agneau à la Maintenon

Poularde du Mans à la Royale

Foie gras à la Périgourdine

Sorbets au Kirsch

Punch à la Romaine

Cailles flanquées d'Ortolans

Canards Rouennais glacés

Salade Rachel

Asperges d'Argenteuil sauce Mousseline

Petits Pois à la Française

Glace Indienne

Gâteaux feuilletés

*The menu for the dinner at the
French Embassy in London.*

Edward kissed Jeanne's hand and told her (in loud French that could be heard by everyone around them), "Ah, mademoiselle, I remember how I applauded you in London, where you represented all the grace and wit of France."

Next day, this little piece of theatrical dialogue was being repeated all over Paris. And meanwhile, all the newspapers published King Edward's speech to the Chamber of Commerce, which warmed French hearts even further. It was a media campaign worthy of the twenty-first century.

Suddenly, the mood of the visit changed. Edward, Paris's favourite Englishman, the world's greatest and most sociable Francophile, was back. On the morning of Saturday, 2 May 1903, the British royal flag was cheered as it was raised above the Hôtel de Ville, a building famous as the scene of anti-monarchist demonstrations in 1789 and 1870. Edward arrived there just before noon, dressed in his red jacket and a feathered hat, and was cheered by a large, enthusiastic crowd. He was greeted as "an old friend" by the city's mayor, and presented with an engraved glass to commemorate his visit. In reply Edward gave a spontaneous speech in fluent French.

Edward told Paris's councillors that: "It would have been vexatious not to have been able to stop at the Hôtel de Ville while I was in your beautiful city. I thank you sincerely for the welcome you have given me today. I will never forget my visit to your charming city, and I can assure you that it is always with the greatest pleasure that I return to Paris, where I am always treated as if I were *chez moi*."

Next day, the French newspapers were unanimous: Anglo-French relations were back on track. *Le Figaro* reported that this was "not only a visit from the most Parisian of Princes … The royal words that we have just heard rang in our ears as the promise of a new era in relations between our two peoples."

In London, *The Times* was much kinder to Edward than it had been in the past, when it had criticized his morals, and now conceded that it had been the King's "Parisian way of living in Paris that won influence for him." Yes, even the staid English establishment was saying that it was acceptable to frequent French actresses and call girls if it was in the national interest. Quite a turnaround from Victorian morals.

Back in Paris, Edward was being cheered wherever he went. On the third day of his visit, at a dinner with President Loubet, he gave a speech of thanks in which he said that: "I have known Paris since I was a child. I have returned many times and I have always admired the beauty of this unique city and the spirit of its inhabitants." He then proposed a toast to "the prosperity and the greatness of France". In the previous thousand years, few if any British leaders had admitted that France might be "great".

That evening, Edward rode by carriage to the Opéra, and the crowds were heard to shout "*Vive Edouard!*" and even "*Vive notre roi!*" ("long live *our* king!").

"

Long live our king

!

Edward VII at the Paris Opera.

When Edward left for England on 4 May, he was given a genuinely affectionate send-off. The press reported that the crowds were "joyous" and "enormous", and hawkers did a roaring trade selling miniature puppets of the King, calling out: "Who hasn't got his little Edward?"

At the railway station, King Edward and President Loubet said goodbye like old friends. And as Edward's train departed towards the English Channel, it was cheered by a crowd that, according to the French newspapers, was "fervent", "passionate" and even "delirious". Émile Loubet was looking very tired, *Le Figaro* said, but he was wearing "the happy smile of a man who has just performed a great duty, and performed it well." Loubet was cheered by the crowds all the way back to the Élysée Palace, a very rare occurrence for any French leader who hasn't just won a battle (and apart from Napoleon, there hadn't been many of those).

The British Ambassador to Paris, Sir Edmund Monson, later reported to the government in London that the success of King Edward's state visit was "more complete than the most sanguine optimist could have foreseen". In the space of a few days, with the help of Émile Loubet, the King had transformed the French from anti-British republicans to relapsed Edward-lovers.

However, not everyone in France had been won over. A newspaper called *L'Echo de Paris* reported that a few niceties between Loubet and Edward VII made no impact on real political relations between the two countries. The right-wing paper *La Patrie* promised its readers that the only true relationship between Britain and France was still "antipathy".

Loubet knew that he had to capitalize quickly on the advances made during Edward's brief visit. So at the end of May he announced that he would be visiting England (though in fact he and Edward had already agreed that a return visit would be necessary).

This was to be Loubet's first-ever trip to London, and the first time that a president of the French Republic would visit England – a symptom of the strained relations that the two countries had always had. And from 6 to 9 July 1903, Loubet was royally received in London.

Émile Loubet of France is welcomed by King Edward VII of England during his visit to London in July 1903.

Arriving in Dover, he declared that he was "coming to this great nation, our neighbour, as a sign of our friendship." In London, he and his Foreign Minister Delcassé were met by Edward VII at Victoria Station, where there was a short welcoming ceremony. The Frenchmen were then escorted in an open carriage through the streets of London. Just as in Paris, soldiers lined the route, but tensions had eased, and there was no heavy military presence to protect the visitors. British public opinion had begun to shift.

The streets were decorated with Union Jacks and Tricolours, and a French journalist seems to have been surprised by the warmth of the welcome, noting that "thousands of spectators gave [Loubet] a remarkably cordial reception."

The procession made for Buckingham Palace, where Loubet took the opportunity to say a political word in Edward's ear. Finalizing the Entente Cordiale was going to be simple, Loubet said: "All it needs is the right turn of phrase." Then, turning to Delcassé and Lansdowne, the two Foreign Ministers, he added, "We just have to let these two gentlemen find it."

On his first evening in London, Loubet was guest of honour at a great banquet at Buckingham Palace, at which politics presided over protocol: in order that negotiations could begin right away, Delcassé was seated directly between Foreign Secretary Lansdowne and

Britain's Secretary of Colonial Affairs, Joseph Chamberlain. Until then, Chamberlain had been staunchly pro-German, having been won over by the Kaiser's blatant flattery during an earlier summit meeting. Delcassé immediately set about winning Chamberlain back.

The banquet became the scene of more convivial speechifying. Edward said that he "hoped Loubet would take back with him to France pleasant recollections of his visit." He added that the reception given to Loubet by all classes proved that "there was a really friendly sentiment among Britons toward France, which being Britain's closest neighbour, should naturally be her best neighbour." He spoke in French, telling Loubet that he would "never forget the reception accorded to me there [in France] recently, and the feelings I expressed were those that I have always felt towards France. I hope that our two countries will maintain the closest relations and the deepest friendship. I drink to the health of the President of France, in the glass that I was given during my visit to the Hôtel de Ville, the glass that I keep as a precious souvenir of that happy occasion."

Loubet replied that: "Your Majesty's words of welcome are all the more important to me because I know they are addressed to the whole French nation. Your Majesty's visit to Paris will produce the happiest results. It has helped to tighten the links between our two countries."

Next day, Loubet was invited to the Guildhall, the ceremonial headquarters of the City of London, by the Lord Mayor, Sir Marcus Samuel. The President was the star of yet another procession through the streets of London, and again a French journalist was struck by the warmth of it all: the reporter writing for *Le Temps* was impressed by a procession "of majestic pomp, taking the head of a large foreign country to the heart of London."

A banner displayed along the route of the procession caught another French reporter's eye. Written in gold letters on a blue background was the word "Marsanne". This was the name of Loubet's birthplace, the village in the Drôme of which his father had been mayor. Displaying the name of such a tiny French community in Europe's biggest metropolis was a highly significant gesture, according to the correspondent of *Le Petit Parisien*, who wrote that: "The aim was to ensure that the President's attention would be drawn to the single word that would affect him the most, one that would evoke the memory of his mother and the small farm in Marsanne. It was clearly a heartfelt gesture."

King Edward was not present at the Guildhall reception, because this was a welcoming ceremony organized by the City of London itself. The Lord Mayor was presiding, and arrived in all his ceremonial garb, including a hat decorated with black ostrich feathers, a gown of purple velvet with an ermine collar, and a heavy gold chain of office.

However, to show royal support for the ceremony, the Prince of Wales, the future King George V, was present, accompanied by his wife Mary. It was a real mark of respect given that this was the first time in history that the Guildhall had ever received a non-royal guest of honour. Even Britain, one of the oldest monarchies in the world, was finally beginning to recognize the sovereignty of republics.

One of the many illustrations published in the French and British press at the time shows Loubet, soberly dressed in a dark civilian suit, being welcomed outside the Guildhall by a horde of Brits in ceremonial costume. The Lord Mayor in his colourful robes, council members in blue gowns, aldermen in red and black, and the librarian in a long white wig. London policemen, wearing swords for the occasion, had received the order to shout out *"Vive Loubet!"*.

This costumed crowd then moved to the Guildhall library, a scene which was vividly described in *Le Temps*: "[The library] is noble, high-ceilinged, vast, and was more than half-full of medieval citizens, gathered there to receive this very modern-looking civilian, Monsieur Loubet, in his simple black suit. Try to picture the slender arches rising like chapels on each side of a nave, all of them full of brown books with titles that stand out like droplets of gold. Imagine the light filtering in through ancient stained-glass windows." It is as if French readers would find it hard to believe the splendour of the ceremony being given in honour of their humble head of state.

In the library, before this crowd of spectators, the Lord Mayor thanked Émile Loubet for the warm welcome given to King Edward in Paris, and began to flatter the French in a decidedly un-English way, talking about a "hard-working people" motivated by "a love of liberty" and possessing more than an average share of "men of genius". He went on to suggest that the preceding centuries of Anglo-French war had been caused by "a few misunderstandings". (Whether this was an example of the famous British sense of humour or an extreme case of amnesia is not clear.) The Lord Mayor then expressed a more realistic hope that the politicians would be able to prevent war between two nations with so many shared interests (notably, of course, their common desire to bash the Kaiser).

Émile Loubet replied with a speech expressing his desire to see "an Entente Cordiale between our two nations that will serve the cause of humanity." Like the Lord Mayor, he also seemed to want to erase the memory of centuries of war and rivalry between Britain and France when he recognized "how much England has contributed to the triumph of the principles of liberty in the modern world." (This just a couple of years after France had been publicly furious about the Boer War.)

After the speeches, everyone, including Prince George, stood up for that anti-monarchist hymn, the *Marseillaise*. There was so much Anglo-French harmony in the air that it was as if Joan of Arc and Napoleon had never even existed.

Loubet was then accompanied to a table on which lay the Lord Mayor's mace and sword of office. There, according to the ironically detached journalist writing for *Le Temps*, the librarian in his Louis XIV wig "told Monsieur Loubet a lot of outdated stories explaining why they were giving him a speech of welcome, contained in a horribly expensive box."

Edward VII had received an engraved glass when he went to Paris's city hall in May. But in exchange, he made sure that London gave Émile Loubet a much more valuable gift, a richly decorated golden casket. And if this small, ornate chest was so "horribly expensive" it was because it had been specially made by the best jewellers in London, the Goldsmiths and Silversmiths Company.

Cast in solid gold, the casket was topped with a statue of Peace presenting laurel crowns to Britain and France. It was further ornamented with diamonds and silver figures, the enamelled flags of the two countries, and the initials of Émile Loubet.

Inside the casket, rolled up on a satin lining, was the "speech of welcome" mentioned by the reporter from *Le Temps*, a parchment inscribed with a text in honour of lasting friendship between France and Britain, as well as Edward and Émile personally.

This speech commemorates, rather forgetfully, "the friendship which has existed unbroken for nearly one hundred years between the two great and neighbouring nations" and flatters "the leading part taken in the beneficent work of the Civilisation of the world by the French people". All this is pretty standard fodder when aimed at the visiting head of state of a close ally, but the speechwriter piled on the warmth, and declared that "we fervently pray that you may long be spared in health and strength to devote your wide experience and exalted talents to the welfare of your country". This sounds like a deeply personal message to Émile Loubet, similar to the "Marsanne" banner displayed in the street. This particular French president had clearly been singled out as a valuable ally.

In any case, the gold casket and its parchment represented a thoughtful, respectful and, yes, expensive gift to a visiting head of state. But the present was also a political and diplomatic symbol of the new closeness between Britain and France, and the friendship and trust shared by Émile and Edward personally.

The casket was all the more historic because as it was being presented to Loubet, the symbols in its intricate decorations were being made political reality. At the very moment it was being handed over, the two foreign ministers, Lansdowne and Delcassé, were at a meeting. The Englishman opened the proceedings by saying to his French counterpart: "Let's talk." After centuries of war and rivalry, these were simple but momentous words.

Allegory of peace.

After the visit to the Guildhall, the French President invited King Edward and his family to dinner at the French Embassy. Loubet sat at the head of the table with Edward to his right and George to his left. It may sound un-French to exclude the ladies in this way, but it was a gesture of continuity, a sign that the friendship between France and the British royal family would be picked up by the next generation.

The dinner menu was long, and included trout, lamb, duck, quail and foie gras. Everything was French except for one dish, Crème Alexandra, the name of Edward's wife. This was exactly the kind of gallant, witty gesture that Edward would have appreciated (even if it was a rather thick, heavy soup).

The whole atmosphere of the evening was good-hearted according to *Le Petit Parisien*, and the King himself "charming, cheerful and smiling … talking frequently with the President, who was very happy with the cordial, open welcome he has received." The two men seemed to have been enjoying the sweet taste of their success, while political advances were also being made at the banquet: the reporter noted that "Messrs Chamberlain and Delcassé never stopped talking." Everything was going swimmingly.

On the last evening of the President's visit, Edward hosted a grand ball at Buckingham Palace, and *Le Petit Parisien* was proud to report that: "Long before the time announced for

Monsieur Loubet's arrival, a large crowd had gathered along the route of his procession, especially around Buckingham Palace. All along the route, the President was greeted by loud cheers." In the space of just three days, Loubet had become a celebrity in London, and there now seemed to be no doubt that British public opinion would support an alliance with France.

But Edward and his team were leaving nothing to chance. Again according to *Le Petit Parisien*'s starstruck correspondent, "never was there a court ball with so many guests" – there were two thousand of them, including all the ambassadors in London and the cream of British aristocracy. The message to both British and French public was clear: the King was treating the President of France as an exceptionally honoured guest. Edward met Loubet personally on his arrival at the Palace and escorted him through the corridors to the ballroom which, in the same French reporter's eyes, outdid "in splendour everything that Monsieur Loubet had seen during his stay in London."

In short, this was a closing ceremony for the presidential visit that was designed to be as festive as royally possible, providing conclusive proof of the friendship and respect that now existed between the two leaders and their countries that had until recently been on the brink of war.

Loubet and Edward were quick to seal the deal on their brilliant diplomatic work. Over the next few months, the politicians hammered out the text of the Entente Cordiale, the alliance that was to be sealed on 8 April 1904, effectively scuppering the Kaiser's dreams of a great anti-French alliance.

When you look at it closely, the Entente Cordiale is not such a cordial agreement after all. In fact, it is a slightly sordid exchange of colonialist promises – Britain would let France keep Morocco if the French gave up their hopes of grabbing Egypt. Britain ceded some territory in Africa in exchange for a part of Newfoundland in Canada, but promised to let the French fish there without interference from the Royal Navy. And other clauses of a similar nature. It wasn't a real alliance as such; it was just a polite agreement by Britain and France not to steal the other's empires.

But in 1904, so soon after Fashoda, the Entente Cordiale was a minor miracle, and its importance is rightly remembered more than a century after it was signed – now that everyone has forgotten the exact clauses of the agreement.

Of course, King Edward and President Loubet don't deserve all the credit for the Entente Cordiale – diplomats like Lord Lansdowne, France's Foreign Minister Théophile Delcassé, and Paul Cambon (the French Ambassador in London) did much of the political preparation for the agreement. Loubet, much more than Edward, followed the advice of his Foreign Minister. But it would be a mistake to underestimate the importance of the complicity between Edward and Loubet, who did the spadework to prepare the political terrain.

Nothing could have been achieved without the private agreement between the French President and the British King. The treaty between Europe's greatest historical rivals would never have been signed if Edward and Émile had not secretly arranged the royal visit to Paris and the presidential return trip to London.

To forge an alliance with Britain, the French government needed the approval of its suspicious voters, and by inviting Edward to Paris, Loubet had given the French the chance to recall their old fondness for the English Prince before politics had raised its ugly head at Fashoda. And using the seduction tactics taught to him by the Parisians themselves, King Edward had charmed the French people into trusting the British. He also managed to bypass the Francophobes and Germanophiles in his own government and show that an English King really could be warmly received in the country that had given birth to Joan of Arc, Napoleon Bonaparte, and a bloody anti-royalist revolution. Loubet's subsequent visit to London had confirmed all these new impressions. And thanks to the two men's public show of personal friendship, they convinced ordinary French and British people that cordial relations between their respective nations were also possible – and not unnatural.

Even so, in 1904 the danger of European conflict, or even a world war, was still very real. The Kaiser continued trying to enrol his cousin Tsar Nicholas II in an alliance against the French, despite the fact that France was linked by treaty to Russia. Edward VII knew that Britain also had to nurture good relations with the Tsar, so that a powerful Anglo-Russo-Franco triangle could be sealed.

However, in February 1904, just before the signing of the Entente Cordiale, Russia went to war with one of Britain's official allies – Japan. Britain declared that it would stay neutral, but the Russians suspected that the Brits were secretly giving the Japanese military aid.

Kaiser Wilhelm did not miss the opportunity to stir up trouble, of course, warning the Russians that they could never trust an Englishman, even if he was a member of the Tsar's family. And his tactic seems to have worked on Tsar Nicholas, who declared that his uncle Edward VII was "the most dangerous intriguer in the world".

Wilhelm charged gleefully into this breach in Anglo-Russian relations. In the summer of 1905, he arranged to meet the Tsar on a yacht in the Gulf of Finland. There, Wilhelm told Nicholas that their Uncle Edward had "a passion for making 'a little agreement' with every country, everywhere" – he was, in short, as unfaithful as a French lover.

Nicholas seems to have believed this propaganda, and promised Wilhelm that "he [Edward] shall never get [an agreement] from me, and never in my life against Germany." At which point, Wilhelm is said to have pulled a pre-prepared Russo-German treaty out of his pocket and got Nicholas to sign it. Luckily for Europe, without a prolonged period of diplomatic negotiations, this improvised treaty was not legally binding, but the threat of the two cousins ganging up on France was as real as ever.

In the end, it was Émile Loubet who intervened to keep the Kaiser at bay. He offered Russia a large loan on condition that Tsar Nicholas signed an alliance with his British uncle. Once again, world peace was preserved thanks to the partnership of Émile and Edward.

Furious, the Kaiser reacted by ramping up his aggression towards the French, and personally undertook one of the most absurd invasions of the twentieth century.

Cruising around the Mediterranean in March 1905, Wilhelm anchored his ship off the Moroccan port of Tangier, and had himself rowed to shore through choppy seas, almost overturning in the surf – he was apparently terrified the whole way. The Kaiser then rode to the Sultan of Tangier's palace on a horse that objected to being ridden by a German invader and did its best to throw him out of the saddle. At the palace, Wilhelm made a speech declaring that he had come to defend Morocco's right to independence from France. This must have confused the Moroccans, who knew that this crazy German was no match for the garrison of heavily armed French troops who would no doubt want to have a say in Morocco's future.

Even so, Wilhelm was delighted with his speech, and when he got back to his yacht, he sent Edward VII an April Fool's joke in the form of a telegram: "So happy to be once more in Gibraltar and to send you from British soil the expression of my faithful friendship. Everybody is so nice to me. Had a delightful dinner and garden party with … many pretty ladies." It sounds trivial, but this was at a time when colonial tensions were at fever pitch, and the mere idea of German ships docking in Gibraltar would have sent a shockwave of panic as far as London.

It seems almost impossible to imagine a world leader mounting a personal invasion of a French colony, and then threatening a British naval port as a joke. But at the time, world politics was a very personal affair.

So King Edward was forced to take the German "invasion" of Tangier seriously, and duly sent a message of support to his friend Émile Loubet and France. This prompted Wilhelm to call his uncle a "devil" and indulge in public criticism of Edward's immorality, giving an interview to the press about the King's affair with his British mistress of the time, Alice Keppel (the great-grandmother of Camilla, Duchess of Cornwall, the second wife of Prince Charles).

In order to prevent a Franco-German standoff over Morocco, Edward and Émile Loubet hurriedly arranged a conference in Algeciras, Spain, in January 1906, at which Britain officially confirmed its support for France in colonial matters, as promised by the Entente Cordiale. Yet again, the two men had preserved the peace.

In the face of this Anglo-French solidarity, Germany was forced to back down. It is said that when the Kaiser heard the news, he had a nosebleed.

Just after the Algeciras conference, Edward lost his great ally Émile Loubet, because in February 1906, the latter's term as President of France came to an end. Loubet retired from politics, quitting the political scene not only with the satisfaction of seeing the Entente Cordiale signed, but also with the magnificent golden casket that symbolized the friendship and political collaboration between himself and King Edward VII.

He was succeeded in office by Armand Fallières, who understood the strategic importance of the Entente Cordiale as well as Loubet, and who visited London in 1908 to strengthen the ties between the two countries.

With France's continued support, Edward VII never stopped working against his nephew Wilhelm and in favour of world peace. And it was of course not until 1914, four years after Edward's death, that Kaiser Wilhelm was able to embark on the war against France that he had been trying to provoke for so long.

However, thanks to the Entente Cordiale, that war was not going to be the pushover that he had imagined.

——— *STEPHEN CLARKE*

To Émile Loubet, President of the French Republic

We the Lord Mayor, Aldermen and Commons of the city of London, in common council assembled, desire to offer you our hearty congratulations on your arrival in this country as the honoured guest of our most gracious King, and we venture on behalf of our fellow citizens and ourselves to tender you a most sincere and cordial welcome, and to thank you for the honour you have done in attending here today.

We would further express the pleasure it gives us to receive in the Guildhall the Chief Citizen of the great and renowned French nation, and to have the opportunity of greeting through you, the French people, and conveying the kindly and friendly feelings which are entertained for them in this country, and we would add the earnest hope that the bonds of mutual amity and esteem may be drawn still closer by your present auspicious visit.

The citizens of London entertain the sincerest admiration for the leading part taken in the beneficent work of the Civilisation of the world by the French people – leaders alike in Literature, in Science, in Arts and in Commerce – and regard your sojourn in this country as the happy augury of the continuance, in conjunction with this country, of that noble work, and the cementing of the friendship which has existed unbroken for nearly one hundred years between the two great and neighbouring nations.

We trust that the blessing of the Almighty God may rest on the united efforts of France and England, in conjunction with the other Great Powers, to maintain the peace of the world, and that sentiments of international concord and sympathy may increase from year to year, promoting the advancement of human progress and the prosperity of the nations of the world.

In conclusion, we fervently pray that you may long be spared in health and strength to devote your wide experience and exalted talents to the welfare of your country, and the fulfilment of the duties of the proud position to which you have been called by the unanimous[2] voice of the French people.

Signed by order of the court,
James Bell, Town Clerk

Guildhall, the 7th day of July, 1903

---

2. A sign, perhaps of the Brits' over-enthusiasm? Or did they really not understand French democracy? No French president, not even De Gaulle, has been elected unanimously.

The golden casket, delicately engraved with symbols and allegories using the distinctive emblems of each country.

HOW TO FIND
THE TREASURE?

HOW TO FIND THE

A TREASURE IS ACCESSIBLE ONLY
TO THE BRAVE.

◆ This treasure hunt was designed so that everyone could participate. Some puzzles are easy, even very easy; others require insight and careful research. On the one hand, this will make it easy for new hunters to take this treasure hunt into their own hands and progress through puzzle solving, possibly finding the location of the treasure. On the other hand, more experienced players will easily solve the first puzzles, but then be slowed down by their increasing difficulty.

This is not an easy treasure hunt.

In order to conquer it, you will need tenacity: a treasure is accessible only to the brave.

- This book. It includes 9 puzzles. Each of these puzzles is made up of a picture and of a poem that is hidden in the tale of the Edrei. The first thing to do is to reconstruct these poems, then to resolve the encryption that allows it to be completed and finally to interpret its indications. A single "_" is a clue to indicate that a part is missing and you need to complete. The puzzles are listed in order.

- The treasure map. It contains secrets that need to be uncovered and will be a real tool in your investigation. There may be times when the map shows you locations on which you need to zoom in or research. No need to go there for additional information: everything is on the internet or in good encyclopaedias.

- The adventurer's notebook. It includes puzzles that will allow you to add details to specific stages of the hunt; it's up to you to find which ones.

You will find all these elements as well as the complete regulations and registration link to take part in the treasure hunt on :

www.thegoldentreasureoftheententecordiale.com

A paper and a pencil will be enough to discover some solutions. For others, you will need to do additional research: as mentioned above, the internet will be a valuable ally in finding the information you need without leaving your chair.

While it takes cunning and ingenuity to solve puzzles, it is above all your perseverance which, pushing you on where others leave off, will allow you to win the treasure! Happy hunting everyone,

———— *M. BECKER AND V. BIANCA*

Happy hunting everyone

Jean Pierre Guilhem

EXPERT JOAILLIER

GEMMOLOGISTE BREVETÉ D'ÉTAT
DIPLOMÉ DE L'ÉCOLE BELGE DE GEMMOLOGIE, EXPERT CNES
EXPERT PRÈS LA COUR D'APPEL, LES DOUANES,
LES COMPAGNIES D'ASSURANCES
MEMBRE DE L'ORGANISATION INTERNATIONALE DES EXPERTS

EXPERTISE D'UN COFFRET EN OR
par (Goldsmiths & Silversmiths Company Ltd)

Le coffret présenté est une pièce exceptionnelle, dont il ne fait aucun doute, tant à l'historique qu'à la fabrication superbe du créateur, Goldsmiths & Silversmiths Company Ltd, orfèvre de sa majesté le roi.

Au printemps 1903, le roi d'Angleterre Édouard VII entreprend l'un de ses plus importants voyages en France. Il rencontre le Président de la république Française, Emile Loubet pour signer un accord réglant les différents coloniaux entre le Royaume Uni et la France et empêchant toute future guerre : les bases de l'entente sont posées. L'accord est signé le 8 avril à Londres, par Petty-Fitz Maurice et l'ambassadeur français Paul Cambon.
Le coffret offert au Président Émile Loubet le 7 juillet 1903, commémore cet accord de paix entre les deux états, scellé au printemps de la même année et signé sous la forme d'un pacte, à Londres, le 8 avril 1903.
Les attributs et symboles de ce présent figurent l'entente cordiale et la paix qui président entre la France et le Royaume Uni.

La matière est de l'or 750/1000, soit 18 carats, ce coffret possède des poinçons qui le confirment.
Son poids est de 1 kilo 450 grammes.
Il ne comporte pas de coup.
Les diamants taille rose sont intacts, ainsi que les parties émaillées de grande qualité.

Le coté exceptionnel de l'objet n'ayant pas de comparaison dans les dernières ventes publiques en France et à l'étranger ne nous permettent pas de le référencer, mais nous pensons que la valeur se situe autour de 750 000,00 euros (sept cent cinquante mille euros)

PJ : Documentation annexée à la présente expertise
(Victoria & Albert Museum, Musée du Nouveau-Brunswick)
concernant quatre coffrets provenant
de Goldsmiths & Silversmiths Company, orfèvre à Londres.

Fait à Béziers, le 15 janvier 2015

Guilhem Joailliers
11, rue du 4 Septembre · 34500 BEZIERS
Tél. 04 67 28 34 05 · Fax 04 67 28 29 73

S.A. au Capital de 250.000 F · R.C.S Béziers B 321 315 517
SIRET 321 315 517 00011 · N° TVA FR 42

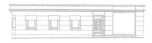

The official expert appraisal of the golden casket.

The enamelled-silver coat of arms of the City of London, decorated with two griffons and a helmet bearing the city's motto: "Domine dirige nos".

PRESENTED BY
THE CORPORATION OF THE CITY OF LONDON
TO
MONSIEUR EMILE LOUBET
PRESIDENT OF THE FRENCH REPUBLIC
WITH AN ADDRESS OF WELCOME
ON HIS AUSPICIOUS VISIT TO ENGLAND
AS THE GUEST OF
HIS MAJESTY KING EDWARD VII.
GUILDHALL, 7TH JULY 1903.

A small plaque engraved with an inscription from the City of London and Edward VII, addressed to President Emile Loubet of France.

Detail of the golden casket showing the hallmarks of the jeweller, the crown of the United Kingdom and the amount of 18-carat gold contained in the casket.

THE TREASURE
OF THE EDREI

1 In the beginning

In the beginning there were the heavenly twins: Nehemah[1], the Creator and Kaguluhan[2], the Destroyer. Nehemah was female, Kaguluhan was male.

From **their** embrace the world was bor**n**.

While the **G**oddess created in abundance, t**h**e God took aw**a**y the **s**urplus th**a**t would have **s**tifled life.

The Edrei[3] were the first cre**a**tures to exist. Child**r**en of **t**he clouds, they lived clo**s**e en**o**ugh to heaven to be aware of the **d**ivine presence. Behind each th**o**ught, each ray of sun**l**ight, each drop of r**a**in, **t**hey _per**c**eived Nehem**a**h**'s** power and heard **t**he distant echoes of her joyful h**ea**rt. As soon as t**h**e Edr**e**i appeared, they thanked the **G**oddess for her benevolence by devot**i**ng an endu**r**ing cult to her. But more than anything, they feared the wind of Kagu**l**uhan, the only thing capable of de**s**troying t**h**eir frail b**o**dies made of clo**u**ds.

One day, they descended to Earth: and thus began the era of humankind.[4]

---

1. Nehemah means "Our mother" in Navajo.
2. Kaguluhan means "Chaos" in Tagalog, an Austronesian tongue, the national language of the Philippines.
3. E**d**rei: a bibli**c**al name me**a**ning "Cloud".
4. **T**he footnotes in**c**luded th**r**oughout the text will help **you** to att**r**ibute - thanks to th**e** highl**y** subj**e**ctive knowle**d**ge of the auth**o**r - new mean**i**ng **t**o certain myths and legends. It's no **bother** at all for me **her**e, as a **he**lpful Footnote, to pass on th**is** knowledge and thereby he**l**p y**o**u t**o** progress by unlin**king f**act fr**o**m fabrication. **Th**is m**e**ans that you must **read** me carefully. You will be doing yourself a **kin**dness and making me feel **g**ood about myself.
It's up to you: **will you dare to** read and believe all these rewarding **foot**no**tes? On **the other** hand, looking at things from my **side**, is there really **a** secon**d** option? So t**ake you**r time, conside**r** what I say and believe me, **we** are go**ing** to have fun. The Footnote

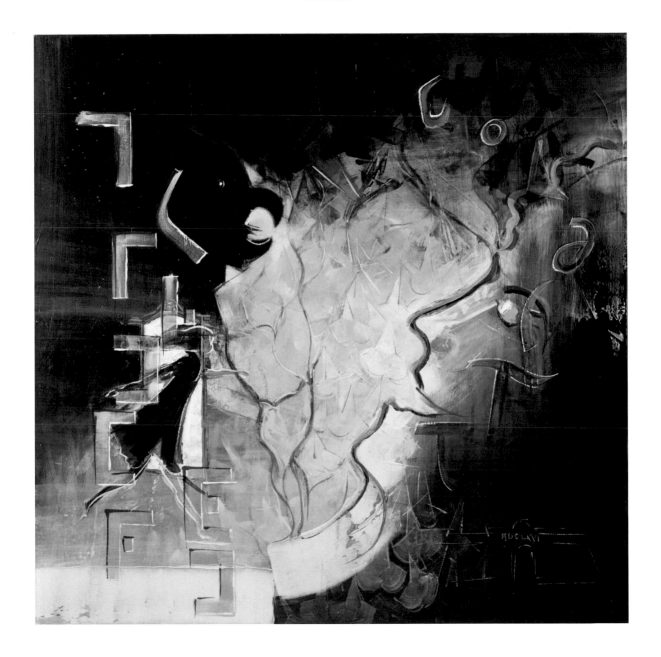

2 The origin of the clans

From **t**he beginning, the Edrei were divided int**o** two clans: the Albians[5] and the Phrygians[6]. To both, time was meaningless: past, present and **f**uture c**o**-existed in a coherent and constant who**l**e. However, the Goddess had created the two clans to be un**l**ike each **o**ther: and this they **w**ere, each persuaded of **the**ir own sup**e**riority. Their enmity w**a**s as much par**t** of **t**heir being as the energy flo**w**ing through their bodies.

Although similar in man**y** respects, with their nebulous limbs, made up of smoke that stirred when the**y** sp**o**ke, the Albians differed from the Phrygians in one tiny detail, which they regarded as profo**u**ndly important: the spirit of the P**h**rygians, their head so to speak, ended in a rounded tip that the Albians liked to c**a**ll crumpled. The Albians in turn boasted of their sharp brain, ending in a cur**ve**d tip, **t**he narr**o**wness of which the Phrygians were always quick to point out.

The concept of **m**an and woman did not **e**xist amongst the Edrei: they sw**a**pped orientation, each according to their personality, between characteri**s**tics that today are considered specific to one or other sex.

The Edrei were not born in the sense that we **u**nde**r**stand: th**e**y simply appeared, and the place where they emerged bro**u**ght them clo**s**er ei**the**r t**o** the Albia**n**s or to th**e** Phrygians. The elders w**o**uld quickly instruct newcomers in how to pray to the Goddess, explaining how the

---

5. Albion comes from Ancient Greek; it is one of the ancient names of Great Britain.
6. The Phrygian cap is one of the French Republic's most important symbols.

opposing clan was in error. Sometimes the elders looked for traces of divine marks in the smoky wisps of the newly created Edrei. The most innocent claimed that they hoped in this way to contemplate a fragment of the Goddess's beauty. Others admitted that, by these examinations, they were trying to find proof of the ineptitude of their eternal adversaries.

Endowed with the power of metamorphosis, the Edrei used it as a survival technique: their bodies were light and airy, and could not maintain their concrete form indefinitely. To replenish their energy, the Edrei were obliged to take on the form of earthly beings. In this way, travelling the world, they gathered the strength necessary for them to survive and worship the Goddess. They thus alternated their phases of existence between the clouds and the Earth.

The Albians, who were organized and methodical and who enjoyed the peacefulness of a carefully thought-out society, would materialise as plants. The Phrygians, on the other hand, were lovers of intense, short-lived passions, and preferred to metamorphose into animals. Each Edrei remained in their chosen earthly form for as long as necessary before returning to their own shape, up beyond the clouds. As long as they stayed away from the wind of Kaguluhan, they were immortal, but they became vulnerable while they were metamorphosed, and so exercised great caution during their periods of mutation.

In their natural state, the Edrei lived at such great altitude that they could not see the Earth. The Albians loved the fullness of the altostratus clouds that melted into the horizon; the Phrygians preferred the more outlandish forms of the cumulonimbus.

The Edrei only assembled their whole clans on special occasions – solstices, eclipses and other events demanding that they pray to the Goddess. And they differed in their style of worship as in almost all other aspects. Adhering to the spirit of worship rather than the letter, the Phrygians had their own interpretation of each of the Goddess's commandments. It was said that she breathed through the Edrei: thus, the Phrygians believed that their Creator lived through them, and therefore that even the smallest of their acts was divine, so that they were right about everything. The Albians, on the other hand, considered themselves servants of the Goddess, and believed that they should question their every gesture in an attempt to meet her lofty standards.

Their styles of worship were shaped by these differences. Led by their monarch, the Albians meditated in silence, concentrating on the vapours of their bodies. The Phrygians, inspired by their representatives, favoured loud speeches and the singing of hymns.

"The Goddess breathes through the Edrei," the Phrygians' preacher repeated tirelessly. "Each of our breaths pays tribute to her, and everything we do is good."

The Albians' preacher held the opposite view: "Her breathing is a metaphor," he said. "We must not take the word literally. It means that everything we do must pay homage to the Goddess."

Hence the two schools of belief were in perpetual opposition, sometimes leading to earthly combat when words were not strong enough.[7]

---

7. One of the main differences between Catholics and Protestants lies in their interpretation of the Eucharist. Catholics believe that the host and the wine "really" become the body and blood of Christ during communion. Protestants believe it is a symbol. This is one of the reasons why they repeatedly resorted to killing each other over the centuries.

3 The day of the eclipse

_On one occasion, during a perfectly normal eclipse, their rivalry boiled over. Neither clan wanted to stop praying as long as the other continued. Gathered as close to the sun as possible, they roused themselves into a frenzy of competitiveness, invoking the Goddess for so long, and with such ardour, that she diverted her attention from the creation of the world.

Then the wind of Kaguluhan blew harder.

Unpredictable and variable, this wind that the Edrei feared blew into the heart of the distracted Goddess. She ejected it, but not quickly enough to prevent it from creating a teardrop in her heart. A tiny black teardrop.

That day, the world as the Edrei knew it began to change. The Earth, until then a verdant paradise, lost some of its splendour. The first Edrei to metamorphose soon realised this. The air was no longer as fragrant, the sun as soft or the water as clear. The plants withered, stones crumbled to dust, animals disappeared, swept away by the wind of Kaguluhan.

Soon, the pernicious wind attacked the clouds. Once plump and perfect, they grew thin and ungainly. The Edrei looked on powerlessly as growing swirls of cloud flew away from their ancestral homes. The Edrei had to be careful not to be evaporated themselves.

The wind blew so strongly and incessantly that the Albians and the Phrygians were forced to live side by side, even though their mutual hatred had never been so fierce. In the hope of restoring the wounded Goddess's strength, they prayed even more fervently than ever; they invoked, begged, performed endless rites – but all in vain.

THE DAY OF THE ECLIPSE

The once communicative Goddess remained silent.

Even the days were fading: the sun shone less brightly, contrasts became dull, life was losing its colour.

No one knows whether the Albians or the Phrygians struck the first blow, but everyone is aware of the disastrous consequences of the conflict that it started. Unable to fight in their natural form, the Edrei made Earth their battlefield. Peaceful leviathans began to uproot forests. Flowers were trampled by wild beasts, tree branches fell on the smallest animals, deep-rooted vines began to strangle everything they touched. In this way, the Albians hoped to kill off the Phrygians, and vice versa. They believed that the victory of one would prove the responsibility of the other for creating the catastrophe that nothing seemed able to stop.

Armies of Phrygians used wildlife as bait. Masters of the seas, they attacked the seaweed and managed to drive out the Albians, who took refuge in the forests, and dug in there. Meanwhile, herbs, flowers and bushes attacked the animals that they had previously fed. In a panic, both fauna and flora began to adopt strange behaviour patterns. They fled towards the wind of Kaguluhan while convinced they were escaping it, they killed those they were trying to help, and perished en masse in the service of a cause that they did not fully understand.

The carnage reached such heights that the Goddess began to grumble. As the battle raged on Earth, thunderclaps echoed in the clouds. Lightning flashed, silencing the preachers of both camps. Warriors were torn out of their metamorphosis and thrown into chaos. The heavens were ripped apart by a barrage of hail; the barriers that protected the Edrei from the wind of Kaguluhan threatened to give way.

Albians and Phrygians no longer knew where to turn their tormented bodies. Tossed about by the storm, they bumped into each other, merged, shouted, and the most recently born even forgot the names. The world had lost all meaning, and the unthinkable was happening: ivy pierced the clouds, its stems swarming with huge ants who were not afraid of the chaos. The Edrei tried in vain to hide under the leaves or behind the insects; and they no longer managed to metamorphose.

When their terror was at its peak, and they believed their final hour had arrived, the Goddess became calmer. In the subsiding chaos, her fury turned into a litany that everyone could hear:

"FOLLOW THE IVY PATH, MY CHILDREN.
AT THE END A TREASURE WILL LIE
THAT WILL SAVE YOU IF YOU UNIFY.

IN THE ELEMENTS, FOUR ARE AS ONE:
GOLDEN RULE, THREE OF EACH TO THEM SHALL FLY!
HURRY ALONG THE IVY PATH, MY CHILDREN.

Confusion reigned among the Edrei. Thanks to their divine nature, it was not difficult for them to understand the Goddess's words: their meaning was clear. However, the difficulty was to accept the implications of her words, which the permanent nature of the ivy path impressed upon them. The ivy had seemed to grow at random during the storm, but it now stretched out in a single stem that began at the Edreis' cloud, before disappearing into an ocean of whiteness. Its shimmering green leaves and busy ants were reminiscent of the ancient face of the Earth, before the wind of Kaguluhan blew too hard.

The Albians and Phrygians held a council. The ruler of the Albians brought his faithful entourage, and the Phrygians sent their elected representative and his ministers.

"The Goddess has spoken," the Albian declared. "To save her, three emissaries from each nation must follow the ivy path."

"There is a meaning hidden in her words," the Phrygian replied. "We must reach the four elements, that much is clear. Water, air, fire and earth will help us find the treasure that will save us. However, this is a test, not an alliance: the victorious faction will become masters of the Edrei. Any union between us would be unnatural!"

"Your words merely foretell your own defeat!" the Albian retorted. "Let the selection begin."

Each nation used its own methods to choose its emissaries for this vital quest. Without any hint from the Goddess as to the qualities needed for victory, they had to rely on their own judgement.

The ruler of the Albians, who favoured balance above all things, chose Elk[8], a fearless warrior, Ute[9], the wisest of all Albians, and the cunning Moasi.[10]

The Phrygians took much longer to decide. Eager to choose equitably from the best candidates, they held several elections in order to select three names with as much objectivity as possible.

The Albians grew impatient during their adversaries' long prevarications and began the quest as soon as their royal selection was made.

---

8. The French word for "elk" – "élan" – also means "vigour" or "speed".

9. Ute means "Native American" in Navajo.

10. Moasi means "cat" in Navajo.

4 The Albians and the fire geode

The ivy stem was wide enough for Ute, Elk and Moasi to walk side by side. Never before had they felt so tiny, or so unlike a plant. The ivy seemed to possess a life of its own, familiar and yet radically different to theirs, as if the Goddess had instilled it with her deepest power_.

Its large leaves formed steps, upon which the three smoky silhouettes floated. They progressed slowly through the clouds, from one level to the next, never able to see the end of the gigantic stem which disappeared over the horizon. Tirelessly, the ants followed them in an unbroken line. Days and nights passed, and no Phrygian caught up with them.

"How slow they are to decide!" Elk said. "Even when the very survival of the Goddess depends on their decision, they are unable to hasten their cursed elections."

"They have always been lazy," Moasi hissed.

"Remember the War of Worship," added Ute. "When our first monarch had the revelation of the Goddess and opposed the noisy prayers of the Phrygians. They accused us of treason, and said we no longer deserved to be called Edrei!"

"Did you exist at that time, Ute?" Moasi asked.

"I appeared very soon after that period."

"And what about the big schism?" Moasi went on. "Was there ever a time when the Edrei were one nation?"

"That's a legend," Ute said. "The Phrygians are inferior to Albians, you just have to look at their

slender forms to realise it. The Goddess wanted a single people, otherwise we would not share the name of Edrei. But the ignorant amongst us dithered, and made illogical interpretations, and the Phrygians were born."

"You talk too much," Elk cut in. "Look! The ivy path climbs into the sky, but there is another branch plunging towards the Earth. We must hurry!"

Trailing in the wake of their impetuous companion, Ute and Moasi flew faster. The leaves barely shimmered as they passed, and their concentration made their silhouettes sharper than ever, accentuating the tip of what looked like a helmet that harboured their most intense thoughts.

Elk was not mistaken. In the middle of the sea of clouds, the gigantic ivy stem split in two. One stalk rose into the sky, while another plunged down into the clouds; the ants were following the latter. The clouds were billowing around the ivy, blown by the wind of Kaguluhan. The Albians were careful to stay close to the divine plant, which was motionless despite the deadly breeze.

"Which path shall we take?" Elk asked.

"The sun is the origin of all life," muttered Ute. "We must go there first."

Climbing up the ivy was no more difficult than following the gentler path that had led them above the clouds. Consisting only of smoke, the Edrei did not need to obey the laws of gravity; they moved easily in any direction. So, leaping from leaf to leaf, they sped onwards, climbing higher and higher, until the sea of clouds became a vaporous and distant mist below them.

Soon they were able to see the curvature of the Earth. They knew the planet was spherical, but their keen eyes could see that it was very slightly deformed. Perched on the ivy which rose straight up into the sky, Ute, Elk and Moasi could feel the force of Kaguluhan that was slowly swallowing the planet. Atom after atom, the brother was annihilating the creation of his sister.

For the first time in their lives, the Albians experienced fear. Not the panic they had felt when the Goddess had been angry, nor the not-unpleasant thrill that ran through them during their battles against the Phrygians. While metamorphosed into trees or seaweed, they had repeatedly diced with death; battered by the Goddess's thunder, they had thought that their time had come.

But now they were facing nothingness. Their existence as individuals and their personal errors no longer mattered. The deformation of the Earth represented something so colossal that their vaporous bodies froze in pure terror. One could not fight Kaguluhan. One could only let oneself be engulfed, and sheer helplessness paralysed one's every thought. Kaguluhan destroyed hope before it was born; he annihilated the will to live.

After seeing their potential fate, Ute, Elk and Moasi no longer spoke of the Phrygians. Their battles felt like childish squabbles. The manner in which they were moving along the ivy path changed. They were no longer jumping from leaf to leaf with the energy of enthusiasm. They did not think of their people, their mission, or their glory if they triumphed. The Goddess's ivy had become the thread which bound them to life, their only possible salvation. Following it was now a matter of survival.

As they climbed, they felt the wind of Kaguluhan strengthen. The ivy rose towards the sun, as motionless as ever. Ute, Elk and Moasi could now see the space around the Earth. Their cloud was just one white patch among many.

They no longer dared to float. Clinging to the ivy, they were terrified of being swept away by Kaguluhan if they let go. They were climbing along the plant, like snakes of smoke wrapping themselves around its stem, their thoughts arrowing ahead of them. They no longer spoke or rested. They felt their energy dwindling and feared the moment when they would have to metamorphose so as not to disappear. But had the Goddess restored this power to them?

Travelling through space felt infinitely long to these beings for whom time did not exist. They had never been so far away from Earth, had never kept their natural form for so long without interruption.

Twice, Ute and Moasi stopped moving. Their silhouette was losing its consistency, some of their wisps were in danger of being blown away by the wind of Kaguluhan. Paralysed with fear, they forgot the importance of their mission, and both were on the verge of letting go of the ivy, as if they wanted to allow themselves to be swept away.

Each time, Elk saved them. He enveloped them in his protective smoke, gave them courage, breathed hope and determination into them. He inspired them with his belief in his infallibility, shared his strength, and invigorated them so that they could carry on.

Without Elk's energy, Ute and Moasi would never have reached the sun. They would not have experienced the terror and rapture of those who witness the solar explosions at close range – the incessant, blinding, swirling orange fire, the sudden bursts of red, the raging winds, energy in its purest form, capable of creating anything, and destroying everything.

For a long time, the Albians contemplated the sun. This divine invention of the Goddess appeared to them in all its complexity: immense, impenetrable, uncontrollable. They had ventured as close as possible. The wind of Kaguluhan was no longer blowing: the sun was pulling them towards its centre, and it was all they could do to resist its attraction.

"What shall we do?" asked Moasi.

"The Goddess spoke of a treasure," Ute replied. "We have come to the element of fire: the sun. In it, we must find the means to save ourselves from Kaguluhan."

"I cannot imagine us simply grabbing a flame and leaving," Moasi quipped. "I am suffocating. I feel as if I am melting, even though I have no solid body to melt!"

"The ivy path leads straight towards the sun," Elk observed. "We must follow it. We cannot go back!"

"If we go on without metamorphosing, the sun will suck us in," protested Ute. "It burns the trees and all vapour disappears in its presence. We have to transform."

"We were created by the Goddess, so how could the sun destroy us?" Elk argued. "Even if its heat is very strong, I am sure I can withstand it. Changing shape might make us miss something! And what kind of metamorphosis would be of any use here? Anything vegetable would burn. We must go on in our true form."

"Let's try to merge with the ivy," Moasi suggested. "Its divine nature will protect us. If we feel something inside the sun, we can always go out and see what it is."

THE ALBIANS AND THE FIRE GEODE

Elk and Ute agreed.

Never before had the Albians combined in the same metamorphosis or merged with an existing being. It was not in their nature to unite into a single entity.

Predictably, their first attempts ended in failure. Possessing a life of its own, the ivy rejected their intrusion. It was like trying to melt in water or air, which was beyond their capabilities: the Goddess did not allow them to merge directly with the elements.

First, they tried to unite as a single plant in which their three spirits would co-exist.

But it was difficult, a real balancing act. If one of them made a mistake, the plant would disintegrate. Linked by a tenuous thread, their minds struggled to maintain the connection. It required a single thought, a united desire, a constant force. Any hint of individuality would break their harmony; any personal initiative posed a threat. They had to open up to others like never before; to free their minds and bodies in order to create an entity greater than any one of them.

After countless failed attempts, they managed to form a single, viable vegetable being. They then learned to climb from leaf to leaf without falling or losing their sense of direction. They could not try to grow independently towards the sun; they had to follow the ivy path very closely.

When they were able to unite closely enough to guide the plant with a single will, they tried to merge with the ivy. What had seemed impossible as individuals was achieved by the three of them together without the slightest difficulty.

They were surprised to feel the foreign sap carrying them with it, the blood of the immense being into which they had merged. If they had not rehearsed beforehand, they would have been ejected immediately. But the ivy stretched on, plunging into the sun, and they could not retreat. They felt the heat of the divine star, its lethal energy; to leave the protective stem would mean instant death.

The ivy was so immense that they could not extend their consciousness as far as its roots or its tip. Unaccustomed to this feeling, it seemed to them as though they were reliving their first-ever metamorphosis, when the flood of new sensations had prevented them from concentrating on a single idea.

Several times along the way, their spirit was almost swallowed up in the divine power. In turn, each prevented the other from straying by communicating their thoughts, and this continuous interchange gave them the fragile balance that they needed in order to move forward.

But as they crossed the centre of the sun, Elk broke the harmony. He decided that they could not leave without taking something that would bring them closer to the treasure: a perfect fragment, in the Goddess's image, which would be found at the very heart of the divine star.

Ute and Moasi tried in vain to restrain him. But he jumped out, and instantly vanished in the heat of the sun. At the same time, the suddenly unbalanced Ute and Moasi collided with a stone, which they grabbed like a lifebelt, dragging it along with them over the ivy. The mineral allowed them to restore the harmony they had just lost; it took Elk's place in the circle of their thoughts.

Borne along by the ivy's sap, and numbed by the heat, it felt to them as if an eternity elapsed before they left the sun. They were unaware of crossing space and returning to Earth, of passing through clouds, and the change of atmosphere. They did not realise that they were emerging from the ivy; they felt as though they had never left the ground and had just been lying there unconscious in the stultifying heat.

They did not know if they left the ivy of their own volition or had been expelled. They had forgotten their names, the nature of their quest – and it all took a long time to come back to them. Elk's absence did not concern them, and they were not curious about the strange stone lying next to them.

They lay on the ground, shapeless, tiny smoke creatures alongside the large ivy leaves.

5 The Phrygians and the water geode

Jacass[11], a smooth talker, Lin[12], a precise thinker, and Ganji[13], who did everything in moderation, moved along the ivy path. Elected by their peers after countless arguments, the three Phrygians struggled to catch the Albians, who were a long way ahead_. But the Phrygians felt their presence and made sure to place their wisps on leaves that had not been touched by their rivals.

"More haste, less speed," Jacass stressed. "Those woodenheads probably got lost."

"Do not be so sure," Ganji retorted. "The Albians may be less thoughtful than we are, but they are still Edrei, and therefore just as receptive to the word of the Goddess."

"They're degenerate Edrei, you mean," Jacass replied. "Beings who presume to tell everyone how to behave and who refuse the slightest pleasure. We used to be united, but some of them could not stop themselves behaving differently from their fellows. Their silent way of praying to the Goddess embodies the pure spirit of contradiction. They are the originators of the great schism. They aroused the evil that is eating away at the Goddess. Their stupidity and their pride know no bounds."

"And with your incessant complaining, you illustrate exactly what they think of us," Lin said. "They see us Phrygians as talkative beings who are permanently dissatisfied despite our good fortune. Let us prove them wrong."

---

11. This word is a pun combining the English "jackass" with the French verb "jacasser", meaning "chatter".
12. Lin means "horse" in Navajo.
13. In the Navajo language, "Ghan-jih" means "half".

THE PHRYGIANS AND THE WATER GEODE

Lin accelerated. The constant pace of the ants frustrated her: she wanted to move as fast as the wind of Kaguluhan. She had been elected by the other Phrygians because of her efficiency, and she was determined not to disappoint them. Her rounded head was curved like a cap that asserted her will.

When the ivy path split in two, Lin was in the lead, and stopped. Jacass and Ganji joined her. A little further ahead, the clouds engulfed the shimmering green of the divine plant, while a second stem rose straight up into the sky.

"The ants are going down to Earth," observed Ganji. "Let us follow them; they are our best guides."

"The Albians took the other route," Jacass pointed out. "They are going to the sun, how presumptuous! That branch is a decoy, and they fell into the trap."

Climbing down the ivy stem proved more difficult than moving along it over the clouds. It was not a problem of gravity: the wind of Kaguluhan had picked up, and the Phrygians were forced to hold on to the ants so as not to be swept away. The black insects descended the motionless stem at an unchanging speed, indifferent to the thick white mist swirling around them, and to the temperature, which was falling.

Despite their ethereal nature, Jacass, Lin and Ganji soon began to feel the cold. The swirls of their thoughts moved more slowly; some materialised in droplets that the icy wind of Kaguluhan immediately carried away. The Phrygians began to fear for their lives.

They tried to assume the appearance of ants, but ants did not live at these latitudes. The

Edreis' legs struggled to move, and the divine insects jostled them mercilessly. Without Lin, who usually excelled at metamorphosis, Jacass and Ganji would have been thrown off the vine.

When they finally reached the surface of the Earth, in the form of tiny midges clinging to the belly of ants, it was clear that they were at one of the poles. Before them lay an undulating white landscape that would have been blinding if the sun had not been obscured by a sea of clouds carried on the wind of Kaguluhan.

The ice was deserted. At the inhospitable tip of the world, Kaguluhan had met no resistance. The animals living here were among the first to disappear.

The ivy path crossed the ice and sank into the ocean. The Phrygians were still high enough above the ground for this to be an apocalyptic vision; it looked as if all life disappeared into a black hole.

The blizzard was growing fiercer, threatening to unhook them from their precarious perch. Supremely indifferent, the ants raced straight towards the waves. The Phrygians knew that if they remained in insect form, they would die as soon as they entered the icy ocean; but if they returned to their original form too early, they would be swept away by Kaguluhan's storm.

Huddled together on a worker ant, they prepared themselves for the impact, and became Edrei the moment they hit the water.

Hoping that the fish had been frightened away by their ghostly apparition, and not exterminated by Kaguluhan, the Phrygians did not stray from the ivy. They followed the divine ants, and soon felt a current trying to tear them from the protection of the Goddess.

"Kaguluhan is everywhere," Jacass moaned. "If we become fish, he will take us away."

"Let's continue using the same ploy," Ganji suggested. "Let's cling on to the ants in the form of microorganisms. We will not travel very fast, but we will not cease to exist."

"That cannot be what the Goddess expects from us," Lin protested. "Did we inherit the power of metamorphosis only to reduce ourselves to microorganisms? A fish will be infinitely faster. We have to take the risk."

"In that case, we have to unite," Ganji said. "Like a lone Phrygian, a normal fish has no chance against Kaguluhan, but if we merge our transformations, we can create a being that the current will not carry away so easily."

Jacass and Lin immediately agreed. At their first attempt, they merged into a three-headed fish with a huge tail.

"Not the most aerodynamic of shapes," Jacass observed.

"But see how fast we are moving!" exclaimed Ganji. "Let's stay close to the ivy, we can always end the metamorphosis if necessary."

The Phrygians descended easily along the plant. The current was growing stronger, but not enough to worry them. Their tail kept hitting the ivy, but the ants did not take offence.

They soon encountered a problem they had not anticipated. Covered by thick ice, the surface of the water was dark; deeper down, it quickly turned pitch-black. The pressure around them told them their exact depth. They were still a long way from the seabed, and the ivy path showed no sign of rising. Soon, they would no longer be able to see the bluish light above the ink in which they were swimming.

"It is impossible to follow the path in these conditions," observed Jacass. "We should transform into electric fish."

"Bad idea," Ganji said. "The current of Kaguluhan is getting stronger. Darkness prevents us from seeing what it is about to do."

"Let us become eels," Lin agreed. "We can wrap ourselves around the ivy without fear of being carried away." Three eels were soon following the ivy path, without dislodging a single ant. But then, the presence of the insects on the slender invisible branch had long become miraculous.

The darkness incited the Phrygians to silence, as they listened out for the slightest noise. The cold around them intensified, growing denser and more impenetrable with every metre. The water seemed to solidify, and the darkness became palpable. The current of Kaguluhan exerted pressure on them without a sound. Locked within themselves, each Phrygian dwelled on his or her own thoughts.

Lin pondered on their quest and its outcome, its merits and the words of the Goddess. Ganji sank into deep reflection, reviving countless arguments about the past, the present and the future. Jacass could not stand the silence. He yearned for his home in the clouds, for the rhetorical jousting of the Phrygians, their praise for the Goddess and the carefree first days of his life.

"We should not be here."

Jacass's words were immediately swallowed up by the darkness. Each movement brought him slightly closer to the bottom of the ocean. Before now, he had never imagined there could be degrees of darkness. The black water through which he was slowly moving was nothing like the bluish liquid near the surface, or even the twilight of the first depths. Here, the slightest sound was like a thunderclap. Ghosts solidified, thoughts took shape: in his Edrei form, Jacass probably could not have endured such psychic pressure. Although, as an eel, perhaps his simpler mind was more easily frightened. He no longer felt the presence of his companions. He was only just aware of the ivy along which he was sliding; the divine path had never seemed so tenuous to him.

"We should not be here," he repeated.

"Jacass, stay focused," Ganji told him.

"Can you hear the voices around me? Can you see the colours?"

"Everything is black."

"The world is not like this. Kaguluhan did not devour everything. I am no longer alone. See this sun shining blue in the depths!"

"Calm down, there is nothing to see. We must continue to follow the ivy."

"Follow the ivy or the ants? The ants have left it, I no longer feel them, this is the wrong path, here is the real world. See this sun shining blue in the abyss!"

"Jacass …"

After remaining silent during this conversation, Lin was about to silence the other two Phrygians when she felt a vibration on the ivy and knew that Jacass had just let go.

"Come back!" exclaimed Ganji. "Jacass, you must not leave, you will lose your way. We are under a labyrinth of rock, I felt it as we were descending. Only the ivy path will get you out again! Remember, Phrygians cannot survive longer than the animals they embody. If you remain metamorphosed for too long, you will **d**ie. Come back!"

"See this sun shining blue in the abyss! Don't you believe me? Grab it!"

Ganji's body was struck by a projectile which almost made her let go of the ivy. She was going to throw it back into darkness when Jacass's voice became threatening.

"Do not throw it away! It is the blue sun. The Goddess demands it."

"Jacass, come back!" ordered an annoyed Lin. "Progress is difficult, so we must not stop. If you do not come back to us, we will abandon you here."

"Leave then," sneered Jacass. "The blue sun is everywhere around me. Kaguluhan can do nothing against me. Go…"

He swam away.

"Jacass!" cried Ganji.

"Hold on to the blue sun, Edrei," replied the increasingly faint thought of Jacass. "Do not let it go, remember…"

"Jacass!"

"The clouds! I am at home again…"

The Phrygian's voice faded away. With all her strength, Ganji clutched the stone which had almost made her lose her way. She would have kept calling Jacass, but Lin urged her relentlessly to keep moving. Sometimes, they heard an echo of disturbing laughter, a sound devoid of logic, the voice of a separate, inaccessible reality. Jacass was wandering in the darkness, moving further away with every moment, losing more of his sanity with every second, convinced that he was praying to the Goddess above the clouds.

Ganji moved without thinking, focussing on the stone that Lin had repeatedly suggested she should throw away. They swam for an eternity before reaching an ocean that was less dark. Surprisingly, the water began to get warmer, and the formerly opaque darkness began to reveal shapes. The ivy seemed to thicken, and the ants were present again.

Ganji and Lin did not rest until they reached a sheltered coral reef, where a few fish remained. It was nothing compared to the life that should have been teeming in these waters, but at least it meant that Kaguluhan had not taken everything.

6 The Albians and the earth geode

Ute was the first to regain consciousness. His wispy forms were suffused with the smell of humus and rustic freshness. Beside him, the stone from the sun retained some of its warmth. Grey and rough on the outside, when turned over, its hollow interior contained a reddish crystal, a weak reminder of the divine star's magnificent colours. Its sharp edge revealed its incompleteness: to complete the hollow geode, three pieces were still missing. One per element…

"Where is Elk?"

Moasi's voice was weak; her youthful mind was slow to recover_.

"Elk has joined the Goddess," Ute replied. "He left the sun too early. The geode was hidden inside the ivy …"

"How can you be so sure? It was so hot. What does this geode mean?"

"It was the thing we were supposed to bring back from the sun. See this radiance, this constant warmth, it is not an innocent stone."

"What is its connection with Elk?"

"He thought he would find something inside the sun. One more second and he would still be with us …"

Moasi did not answer. She listened to the trees growing, to the roots burrowing through the earth, and she heard the absence of birds, of insects, of all creatures except the Albians. Even here,

in this virgin forest, the wind of Kaguluhan was blowing. The ivy path meandered through the jungle, its leaves greener than all the others, almost blinding in this world which was becoming duller with every second. Only the red crystal of the geode gave off a vivid colour.

"The geode appeared when Elk left," she said at last. "Perhaps it was thanks to him that it was there …"

"The will of the Goddess is impenetrable."

"Which means that one of us will not escape from the forest," Moasi added. "A life for a geode. The Goddess takes risks at random."

"Come, it is time to get moving again."

"Without the Phrygians, none of this would have happened! The world would be whole. Elk would still be with us. Life would be a game, as it always has been."

"We must move onwards."

"How can you stay so calm? I remember now, it's all coming back to me. Elk protected our thoughts in space, so that the wind of Kaguluhan would not carry us away. It is thanks to him that we reached the sun. The Goddess should not have taken him back!"

"We have to follow the ivy," Ute stressed.

"It is the Phrygians' fault that all this is happening! Why could they not stop their shouting, cease their foolishness and their exhortations? Why could they not just meditate during the eclipse, as we did? They are the ones who distracted the Goddess's attention. They do not deserve to exist. You are calm now, but have you forgotten how furious with them you were when we were walking above the clouds?"

"And you are furious now – did you learn nothing from this voyage? Have you not contemplated the dying Earth, have you not seen the end of all life beyond Kaguluhan? Do you think all this has been caused by our ridiculous rivalry? *None* of us has been worthy of the Goddess's trust; her entire presence is now concentrated in this endless branch of ivy. I don't care about our two clans' differing interpretations. I will follow the ivy path to the end. It is the only tangible proof of the Goddess's existence, the only demand that she has made of us. If necessary, I am ready to give my life to recover the next geode. I don't care about anything else, as long as I fulfil the will of the Goddess. If you prefer to wait here for Kaguluhan, feel free."

Ute did not let Moasi answer. Realising that in his natural form, he could not transport the geode without over-exerting himself, he became a seed. Then, sprouting so as to wrap firmly around the stone, he stretched himself out along the ground.

Moasi preferred to float as an Edrei. She was moving much faster this way, the quicker to find… What? What were they looking for in the middle of the forest? If the sun represented fire, was this place meant to embody earth? She had explored many places before the present cataclysm: none had looked like this.

As she moved onwards, the vegetation grew thicker. At no time did she see the smallest stream or feel the softest breath of air; increasingly large leaves filled the scene, sometimes obscuring the divine ivy from view. Ferns, mosses, shrubs, orchids, fungi, a dizzying variety of flora co-existed in this impossible climate. Different species of trees intermingled: the trunk of an oak was wrapped in banana leaves, the resin of the pine tree smelled of cherries.

Although in her Edrei form, Moasi could hear the plants speaking. Their contagious exuberance seeped into her vaporous wisps, while their fragrances aroused a gamut of mixed feelings in her. She could feel the presence of each plant around her and longed to join them. And then suddenly she remembered Ute.

In his liana form, he was moving much more slowly than her. Moasi feared that in such luxuriant vegetation, she might lose him: it was better to metamorphose near the ivy and wait for him.

Moasi merged with the forest, plunging roots into the humus. With all her being, she called out to Ute. She had metamorphosed into a small cactus with long spines. She called her companion's name, but the cacophony of plant noise was almost overwhelming. The weak sounds she had heard when in Edrei form had become ten times louder.

Each living being shouted its love of life to the world. The tallest of them, with the tips of their leaves, felt the wind of Kaguluhan, and resisted it by sucking energy from the inexhaustible earth. Other plants were more anxious, but found a way of expressing a degree of happiness by flowering expansively.

"Ute, Ute, Ute," Moasi thought.

The earth had never seemed so fertile. As a cactus, her natural environment was sand and drought; and yet, here, in this luxuriant vegetation, she felt at home. A power she had never felt before flowed in her sap. The fact that a cactus could grow here proved the divine richness of the soil. Every Albian began his or her metamorphosis in the form of a seed, but Moasi had grown to her full height in just a few seconds. She would have liked to express her joy and fear by sprouting a magnificent flower, even if doing so, in the species she had adopted, meant death.

"Ute, Ute, Ute," she thought.

Other roots touched hers. These were sister plants, friends who would stand by her, beings who, like her, feared Kaguluhan. She sensed so many memories, so many lives, so many places on the planet, so many feelings in these creatures who had joined her. If she had become a pine or spruce tree, she would not have had enough time to listen to all of them.

"Ute, Ute, Ute."

Then a deep-rooted creeper struck her, and she resumed her Edrei form. Next to her swirled Ute. Between them lay the geode.

"Ute, Ute, Ute."

Why did she keep repeating this name?

"Moasi."

As soon as she heard Ute's voice, she remembered. Her memories drowned out the sounds of the other plants.

"Ute."

The wisps of her companion became still.

"I repeated your name without knowing why," Ute said. "I was looking for you, Moasi, I no longer felt your presence. Without your name to guide me, I do not know what would have happened. It is a miracle that I have not lost the geode."

"It was the same for me, Ute. Without you I would have forgotten everything. What is this forest? Why are the plants so talkative here?"

"While I was a creeper, my roots tried to hold me back. There were so many thoughts, shouts, and memories. The more I followed the ivy, the more I was pulled forward, towards a spirit that dominates all others."

"I did not stay metamorphosed long enough to hear it."

"This is the primeval tree, Moasi. The oldest plant in the world. Legend has it that its roots emerge as seaweed on the opposite side of the Earth."

"It must hold the geode fragment we are looking for."

Ute and Moasi shared the same fear. If they both metamorphosed, who would call out their names to bring them back to their original form? The forest was less threatening to them than the sun, but it was not exactly hospitable…

However, the answer came to them just as easily as it had done when they travelled to the divine star. As before, they combined their thoughts to metamorphose into a single plant, which curled along the ivy, dragging the sun's geode with it.

In the earth, their minds intertwined in a slow progression. The murmuring of other roots saturated the soil, pushing the Albians to the limits of their shared being. The earth was all around them, crumbly and hard, arid and fertile, topsoil and deep earth, the origin and future of all creatures. The Goddess's ivy traced a golden trail through this ochre ocean, a silent path through the wordless clamour of the plants.

Ute and Moasi did not count the days, the number of leaves they sprouted, or the amount of soil they dug; they grew at their plant pace, carried away by the necessity of the metamorphosis of which they had been deprived for too long. The memory of their quest and the importance of the geode was now like the background noise, a recurring dream, mingling with a reality that they felt sure to leave behind them as soon as necessary.

They did not notice that the voices around them were growing louder, nor that the soil around them was getting denser, becoming ever richer in stories and potential outcomes.

Thus, when they reached the primeval tree, they were both happy and surprised. Ute the wise was happy to be in the presence of one of the Goddess's most sumptuous creations; Moasi was surprised to feel so much power, and to sense so much time all around her.

Their roots felt the beauty of the primeval tree far more acutely than their Edrei senses could have done. The roots revealed this being to them in its totality, from its first sprouts buried infinitely deep in the earth, to the blossoms at the tip of its branches that the wind of **K**aguluhan swept away as soon as they formed. The Goddess's ivy path wound onwards through an inextricable labyrinth of wood and earth. Ute was tempted to leave the ivy and stop to listen to the voice of the primeval tree for a while. Moasi resisted this temptation with all her might, sure that leaving the ivy path would mean certain d**e**ath. Their minds clashed in silent argument, and their disagreement grew with every inch, until it threatened to break their hard-won balance.

"We will access the memory of the world!" Ute said wordlessly to Moasi. "The primeval tree will know how to revitalise the Goddess. And it has lived for so long that it will be able to explain the origin of the conflict between the Albians and the Phrygians. It will tell us why what was once unified is now divided, and where the wind of Kaguluhan ends. What if the blossoms that are blown away by the wind do not die, but are able to grow elsewhere, in another world? And do not forget that the whole memory of the Earth is contained here, in these plants that surround us!"

Moasi, who was less gifted at metamorphosis than Ute, could not answer and communicated only raw emotions – distrust, ignorance, fear, pleading.

When they passed beneath the core of the primeval tree, the place where its seed had once been planted, Ute yielded.

He broke the harmony of their combined metamorphosis, creating a branch in their plant and wrapping himself around the primeval tree.

A second geode became entangled in Moasi's roots, and she felt the presence of Ute fading. He did not evaporate as Elk had done; he faded slowly, his voice mingling with the others, as he became a single plant among millions, his being distilled into a few scattered words left over from his evaporated memories.

Carrying the two geodes with her, Moasi used the fertile soil to grow faster. She fled, if a plant can do such a thing. She darted along, until the ivy stem was once again climbing into the clouds.

Only then did she resume her Edrei form. Her memory was intact. Ute's name had saved her from oblivion…

Next to her, the new geode fragment glowed brownish-green. It fitted perfectly together with the sun stone.

Two parts were still missing, and the Goddess ordered her to go up into the sky.

ℱ The Phrygians and the air geode

Once again in Edrei form, Ganji examined Jacass's stone. Its rough pebble surface concealed a crystalline interior that glowed with every shade of blue. Azure, turquoise, night – there was an interplay of elusive hues in the glow.

"It is a geode fragment."

Ganji's whisper went unanswered. Lin was examining the stone cautiously.

"We are looking for the Goddess's treasure," Ganji said. "Is this stone supposed to lead us there?"

"The words of the Goddess evoked the four elements," Lin reminded her. "I assume that each of them hides a geode."

"So there are three more to find. We will never do it in time …"

"Do not despair so quickly."

"The water took Jacass from us. If each element demands a life, we will fail. How did he know that the geode fragment was hiding in the darkness? He mentioned a blue sun. If he had not left us, we would have crossed the ocean for nothing. Is this how the Goddess wanted it to be? Why did we not share Jacass's vision?"

"You worry too much. Let's continue to follow the ivy."

THE PHRYGIANS AND THE AIR GEODE

The Goddess's path rose out of the water towards the sky. Above the waves, the wind of Kaguluhan was imposing its power ;Lin and Ganji moved with increased caution_. Metamorphosed into birds to carry the geode, they prepared to become reptiles if necessary, so that they would be able to maintain a grip on their only protection.

Before reaching the clouds, the ivy branched off towards the horizon. The air was strangely calm. Lin and Ganji's feathers glistened in moist heat. Each flap of their wings required slightly more energy than the last.

The rushing of the waves was followed by that of the leaves. The breeze whipped the trees into an unprecedented frenzy; the air was full of sound.

The ivy continued to climb. The forests gave way to shrubland. Lin and Ganji were now flying over mountains. The air whistled between the summits, creating a melody that became louder as the Phrygians progressed. It was an indefinable and yet very real music, of great volume. Both intimidating and beautiful, it delighted the Edrei.

Hypnotised by the sound, Lin and Ganji forgot to take turns holding the geode. Locked in Lin's talons, the stone was visible only as a blue glow. In her eagle form, the Phrygian felt the power of the opposing currents of air that whistled between the dizzying peaks. In this grey and white world, the winds that mixed with her breath became more tangible than visible beings.

Trade winds, mistral, harmattan, sirocco, khamsin, chinook, bora, zonda – all the winds converged towards a point beyond the next mountains, at the end of the ivy path along which the ants were marching. The air currents created by the Goddess repelled the wind of Kaguluhan, sending out gusts of life that carried sand, water, cold or heat, according to the place and the season.

When Lin and Ganji flew over the final mountain pass, they realised that turning back was impossible. In the middle of a high plateau framed by a circle of snow-capped mountains, the winds converged in a formidable tornado. Even in the absence of Kaguluhan, it would be risky to metamorphose back into Edrei. No one knew whether an Edrei consciousness would survive such a gale. The geode was in danger of falling and getting lost or broken.

As the Phrygians flew on, the winds grew even stronger. What had looked like a whirlwind from a distance evolved into an air column as wide as a mountain. The top of this tornado widened out until it met the sky in an area of improbable calm. Lin and Ganji had never seen anything so simultaneously beautiful and terrifying.

The updraft was lifting earth, branches and droplets of water that were trapped in its invisible force. Although the foot of the tornado covered a large area of ground, it stayed rooted in the centre of the mountain plateau.

The ivy disappeared into the wall of clouds. Lin and Ganji struggled to stay close to the Goddess's divine path.

"Let us become snakes!" Ganji shouted. "I cannot go on as a sparrow any longer, I'm going to be blown away!"

"If I change shape, I'll drop the geode," Lin protested. "The wind is too strong. It will drag the geode away before my metamorphosis is complete."

In a burst of light, Ganji turned into a gigantic emerald-green python, thicker than the ivy stem. Lin needed no explanation: she allowed herself to be imprisoned in the rings of Ganji's body. In this way, they moved painfully onwards, blinded by the debris blown into their eyes by the raging wind.

They heard animal cries, the howls of creatures that had been torn from the ground and would soon cease to be of this world. They were getting close to the tornado, and the Earth became nothing more than a mass of grey, suffocating air that stole the breath away instead of giving it. Ganji clutched the ivy so tightly that it hurt. She had no doubt that the next geode fragment was in the centre of the cyclone. She swore to herself that the two of them would get there.

"Let go of me!" Lin shouted several times. "I am slowing you down. Take the geode and get to the heart of the hurricane!"

Ganji ignored her. Every inch of progress against this invisible wall felt like a victory to her. How could one be paralysed by air? But nothing was as solid as this invisible barrier.

Suddenly, Ganji felt it: the move she had just made would be her last. She could no longer go backwards or forwards. Lin hung like a corpse between her rings, and her voice could no longer be heard above the storm. A weak current of air flowed towards the centre of the tornado, a trickle that flowed along the ivy. It was too weak to carry a python or an eagle, but strong enough for a sparrow.

"Let's both metamorphose," said Ganji's mind. "Both of **u**s will reach the middle of the **h**urricane."

But Lin stubbornly replied th**a**t it was impossible to change shape, and clung with all her might to the **v**ital geode.

By the tim**e** she understood Ganji's next thought, it was too late. Ganji had **b**ecome Edrei again, and her body of smok**e** created an area of calm around Lin. But it was a short-lived window of opportunity, b**e**cause Ganji's wisps were visibly decomposing.

Lin flew at full speed alo**n**g the ivy, oblivious to the wind, accelerating all the time, and she managed to reach the heart of the hurricane just before Ganji had completely disappeared. The peace and benevolence that Ganji emanated made her disappearance all the more unbearable. **W**hy could the roles not be reversed? Lin wondered. She w**a**s less intelligent than Ganji, and less refined than Jacass; she did not deserve to be this eagle that had pierced the wall of clouds, this creatu**r**e that had finally breached the tornado to reach its quiet eye, while Ganji's fate was to fade into nothingness, dispersed by air, as Jacass had been absorbed by water. And there, within reach of Lin's talons, floated the geode, which a favourable wi**n**d now carried towards her.

It was a stone containing white crystals, with a grey h**e**art that was speckled with mauve. And it was a fragment that fitte**d** together perfectly with the geode from the ocean. But two parts were still missing.

THE PHRYGIANS AND THE AIR GEODE

Lin did not want to dwell on these thoughts. She metamorphosed back into her Edrei form and followed the ivy path to the top of the clouds. Her metamorphosis had replenished her energy, and she easily carried the two geodes in her wisps of smoke.

8 Back in the clouds

An ivy path was hovering in the sky. Black ants roamed across its green leaves. Its deep brown stem looked indestructible, a dark line across an ocean of white cloud. It took a sharp eye to make out the two transparent silhouettes facing each other, wisps in which floated four fragments of coloured geode. Without faces or limbs, their thoughts raged freely. In one silhouette, they materialised in the form of a point; in the other, they took on a swirling curve.

No one could have said how long Moasi and Lin stared at each other.

At last, Moasi broke the silence: "Where are the Edrei? I have followed the ivy path so far. I saw the junction with the branch that leads to the sun. The Albians should be here."

"Our territory is slightly further away," Lin murmured_. "I recognised the clouds when I arrived, but I did not want to admit it. The Phrygians lived at the location of the cyclone. The cries of the animals …"

"… of the plants."

Too complex to be expressed in words, the Edreis' thoughts began to mingle. Each saw what had happened to the other's companions, and each understood that the rest of their kind had gone away. The surrounding clouds still echoed with the sound of their stampede. The wind of Kaguluhan had strengthened, and the Albians had taken refuge on Earth, while the Phrygians had sought their salvation in the air. But the former ended up being entrapped by the primeval tree; and the latter were blown away by the hurricane.

BACK IN THE CLOUDS

Except for Lin and Moasi, the Edrei no longer existed. Their only hope lay in the four geodes which, to their dismay, were still incomplete after so many ordeals. They tried to reassemble them, but without success: a tiny fragment was still missing in the colours of the rainbow that the stone contained.

Only one path remained unexplored: that which led beyond their home. The ivy had previously ended at their cloud, but had continued to grow. It now extended onwards, to follow the wind of Kaguluhan.

"It is all your fault," Lin snapped as they set off. "I can't contain my anger any longer."

"You saw my thoughts, Phrygian. Did not you feel the terror when you saw the distortion of the world caused by Kaguluhan? Conflict between us is pointless."

"Had your kind not wanted to be superior to everything else, the attention of the Goddess would not have been distracted. Our companions would still be alive. You disregard the divine word, and you always claim to be superior to the other Edrei. I can't stand it anymore!"

"What about you, you vain, dissatisfied chatterers? You boast of reinventing the world, but merely stagnate in your own idle rhetoric."

"Who caused the great schism? Who broke the unity of the Edrei by claiming to understand the Goddess better than the elders_? The evil thoughts of the Albians are the cause of all our ills."

"The Albians existed before the Phrygians. It was you who created a new form of prayer, because you were incapable of appreciating the one that the Goddess demanded. The War of

Worship was the logical consequence of the great schism. First there was the division into two schemes of thought, an excuse to interpret everything differently, then came the supreme insult: renouncing silence during prayer."

"Perfidious Albian, denier of truth, you are reinventing history! How many times have honest Phrygians been deceived by your kind? How many promises have you broken, how many selfish, vindictive acts have you committed in the guise of holy morality?"

They listed the wrongs and the reproaches as they moved forwards, and neither wanted to yield. Oh, if Ute, Ganji, Elk or Jacass had triumphed in my place, thought each of them to themselves, the argument would have already been won. They would have overcome their inadequacies. They had the qualities necessary to win over any Edrei.

The two Edrei would still have been confronting each other if the ivy path had not suddenly turned on them.

The divine plant was pointing its last bud towards them. An orange-pink shoot, a crystalline bulb with a mineral consistency.

In one, synchronised movement, Lin and Moasi held the hard-won geode fragments up towards the bud. The four pieces fitted together around the celestial shoot. A light flashed along the joins: the stones became one and shone with blinding brilliance.

Suddenly, Lin and Moasi understood what their quarrels had prevented them from seeing earlier. Around them, clouds were disappearing, carried away by the wind of Kaguluhan, and falling into a bottomless void that was as impenetrable as the depths of the ocean, and as vast as the universe. This was the edge of the distorted world as seen from the sun, the teardrop hollowed out in the heart of the Goddess.

The brightly glowing reconstructed geode had opened up a passage into the abyss, a thread of gold along which the Edrei now rushed. At the end lay the Goddess's treasure. The brightest colours and the most beautiful forms of matter were reflected in the smoky wisps of Lin and Moasi.

As soon as they reached the treasure, Kaguluhan rushed in. The brother had finally overcome the sister's resistance.

Colours and matter flew away in a whirlwind of thoughts and sensations. Soon there would be nothing left. And the Goddess was still crying. More than all their ordeals, seeing this pain finally ended the rivalry between Lin and Moasi. The need to save the being to whom they owed their existence awakened their deepest instincts.

Opening their minds, they accepted the evidence they had denied for so long. The Edrei were one. The Albians and the Phrygians were illusory concepts. Their powers were restricted by their thinking. Leaving behind the sphere of plants and animals, they now united in a monster that the wind of Kaguluhan could not overpower. They had metamorphosed into a wooden dragon that was spitting crystal – an impossible yet real creature, strong enough to protect the Goddess's last treasure: a golden box decorated with a stem of ivy, a casket belonging to the being who united them. Their sharp, fragrant green claws opened the precious box, while their formidable wings beat away in the void.

Repelled from the Goddess, the wind of Kaguluhan could not blow away the words that sprang from the golden casket. Letters were written in the air, to be read in unison by Lin and Moasi:

"BEYOND THE DEEP, SWEET SEA,
UNDER THE FIRE THAT GLOWS SO BRIGHTLY,
IN THE LAND OF CITRUS AND LIGHT,
THROUGH THE SWATHES OF MISTY CLOUD SO SLIGHT,

THE ENEMY PEOPLES HAVE UNITED FOR YOU.
FEAR, DEATH AND MADNESS THEY HAVE BEEN THROUGH,
AS ACROSS THE BRINK OF YOUR BRUISED HEART THEY FLEW.

LISTEN, OH NEHEMAH, GODDESS OF CREATION,
THE TREASURE REVEALED BY OUR NOVICE LIPS' ORATION:

HEAL, OH NEHEMAH, WHOSE TREASURE IS LIFE!"

The Edrei fell silent, and the words poured down on to the Earth in a shower of gold, so luminous that Lin and Moasi had to close their eyes.

9 A new beginning

In the beginning there were the heavenly twins: Nehemah the Creator and Kaguluhan the Destroyer. Nehemah was female, Kaguluhan was male. From their embrace the world was born.

While the Goddess created in abundance, the God took away the surplus that would have stifled life.

Lin and Moasi smiled. They stood in an enchanting garden, far below the clouds. Nothing was left of the Edrei. Much of life itself needed to be rebuilt. The Goddess had given them a final gift.

They were now beings of flesh and blood, new creatures, marking the beginning of a new era. They had lost the gift of metamorphosis. But another gift had been granted to them: a talent that required two hands, ten fingers and one spirit_.

Lin and Moasi had become the first human beings, and possessed the power to transmit life. Inspired by the Goddess, they lived amongst the other terrestrial fauna. Over the centuries, their new people multiplied and reshaped the whole world. Their stories gradually became an infinity of legends inextricably mixing the true and the imaginary.

Although they had united to fight Kaguluhan, Lin and Moasi never managed to wear the same headgear. This character trait was passed on to their offspring, who did their utmost to cultivate this difference despite an obvious resemblance.

Various notions have been passed down to us by the Edrei: knowing how to get along together when it is necessary, for example, and proving oneself just and fair, so as to remain worthy of the Goddess. Although admittedly, over the ensuing millennia people have applied these concepts with varying degrees of success, to say the least.

Only one shared passion still inspires humankind today – the most universal and yet least understood heirloom bequeathed by Lin and Moasi_.

It is the fascination for treasure. Traditionally, for treasure locked in a chest.

But Kaguluhan scattered treasures all over the Earth: sun diamonds on the water, rubies in fire, pearls of dew on the grass, gold that flows from volcanoes, sapphires shining in the stars, and opals in aurora borealis. They are still there, waiting to be discovered.[14]

---

14. You are now at the end. We had a pleasant time all together, didn't we? As a footnote, I hope I showed you some useful references. We footnotes are used to being disregarded. I hope this was not the case here. As Maria Popova said: "Literature is the original Internet – every footnote, every citation, every allusion is essentially a hyperlink to another text, to another mind." So it only remains for me to say goodbye, and leave you with my deepest respect. The Footnote

NOTES